WHILE IN DARKNESS THERE IS LIGHT

Idealism and Tragedy on an Australian Commune

LOUELLA BRYANT

with a foreword by
HOWARD DEAN

D1402043

Black Lawrence Press
New York

Black Lawrence Press
New York
www.blacklawrencepress.com

Book design: Steven Seighman

ISBN: 978-0-9768993-9-6

TABLE OF CONTENTS

Gather ye rosebuds while you may,
Old time is still a flying,
And that same flower that smiles today,
Tomorrow will be dying.

—Robert Herrick

from the Rosebud Farm journal

FOREWORD

In October of 1974, I had quit my job on Wall Street and was enrolled full-time at Columbia University's General Studies program, taking the pre-med courses I had avoided as a political science major in college. I had given up my apartment in the West Village and had moved in with my parents on the East Side.

My younger brother Charlie had left 18 months earlier on a trip around the world. I had last seen him in March of 1973 when he got a ride with one of our childhood friends to Seattle, took a freighter to Japan, and eventually found his way to Australia. There he lived on a remarkable farm being carved out of tropical rainforest north of Cairns. He was with two kids I had known from St. George's School, Kim Haskell and Harry Reynolds. I had seen Kim once since graduation, when he visited me when I was on Wall Street, showing up at the brokerage office unannounced. He was on his way back from Angola to visit his parents in Delaware before going back to Australia. I was shocked by his appearance. He was about six-feet-three with long black hair, a bandana around his head, and a large earring which was pretty out of place for a male in the 1970s. I decided lunch out of the office as fast as possible was a very good idea. I knew Harry less well. He was an all-conference hockey player in high school and had gone on to play at Harvard. I had lost track of him in the intervening years until he surfaced twenty years later as a teacher in Vermont, where I had moved after medical school.

Charlie had left Australia sometime in July 1974, and my family and I received letters from Bali and Malaysia.

We knew he was headed to Nepal to see a friend in the Peace Corps. The last letter I got from him was in August just before I moved back in with my folks. He was in Laos then and talked about how beguiling the Lao were, how gentle they were. He wrote about living in a small bungalow by the Mekong with a friend he had met in Australia, Neil Sharman. He also wrote about the sounds of artillery shells exploding in the night, just beyond the outskirts of Vientiane. I remember wanting to call him (which of course was impossible) and then wanting to write him, telling him he should get out of there now. But I figured he was twenty-four years old, he had been halfway around the world on his own, and he probably knew a lot more about what was going on in Laos than I did.

My family was worried. I cabled our friend in the Peace Corps in Nepal who wrote back in September saying he had not heard from Charlie. Over the next week or so, we tried to figure out our options for contacting him.

One morning around 10:30 I was alone in the apartment getting ready to go up to Columbia when a phone call came for Mr. Howard Dean. Thinking it was for me, I acknowledged the caller who then identified himself and said, "I am from the State Department and we have reason to believe that your son, Charles Dean, is a prisoner of the Pathet Lao in Laos." My reply was short: "I think you had better call my father."

Ten minutes later Dad was on the phone. "How do you like those apples?" he said in his raspy voice. Oddly enough, we were relieved for a while. At least we knew where Charlie was, and we also knew, thanks to an incredible amount of information from the State department and the CIA, where he was being held, that he had been captured on September 14, and that he was in no immediate danger. We even had intelligence reports describing a vegetable garden that he and Neil were allowed to grow to supplement their meager prison fare. We knew that, characteristically, Charlie was learning the language, speaking optimistically, and insisting regularly that he and Neil be allowed to leave. Neil was more withdrawn, but neither was being abused.

All my brothers and I were close. Charlie was 18 months younger than I, and we shared a room for years, he in the top bunk (his choice), and I below. My brother Jim followed four years later, and then Bill, who eventually became the biggest and strongest of us, bringing up the rear a year after Jim.

Charlie and I were great rivals in some ways, as you might expect among the oldest pair of four boys, but we were bound by a special pride my father had instilled in us, and by the occasional oppression of the tough discipline my father also applied. We built forts together in the summer, went to school together in the winter, and later played sports and partied together as we grew up. We hiked and skied in Yosemite and Vermont. He bought a used school bus when he turned twenty-one, and I traveled with him and his friends from California to New York, stopping every few miles to pour yet another five gallons of water into the sieve that passed for a radiator. I stayed at his place at the University of North Carolina between my own wanderings through North and South America. He turned me on to southern music in the form of the Allman Brothers before anyone up north had ever heard of them. I went to bat for him with my father when Charlie did not get into any colleges and considered joining the Peace Corps instead. Charismatic, stubborn, and deeply thoughtful, Charlie was committed to helping others. While I had interesting summer jobs around the country in high school and college, Charlie worked for five summers in a row at Boys Harbor, a camp for under privileged, largely minority students. He got paid little at first and drove home to do his laundry once a week.

At the same time the U.S. government was attempting to negotiate the release of Charlie and Neil, they were bombing Laos. Our efforts and those of U.S. agencies proved futile. In mid-December my father went to Laos. He was there a week, and every inquiry he made was deflected, as were the inquiries of his friend and American ambassador to Laos, Charles Whitehouse. The Lao would not admit to holding Charlie. My father left a package of food and medicine, which the Lao promised to get to him if indeed he was in their custody without their knowing about it.

Two more months passed with no word. My mother went to Laos in February. She came back deeply discouraged. The Pathet Lao representatives would not acknowledge knowing anything. Worse, they would not look my mother in the face. She had had a dream that Charlie had been shot in the head.

In May my father got a letter from the Asia Society which had good relationships with the Southeast Asian communists in all three countries. Charlie and Neil had been killed, most likely around the time my father had been there.

My father, who for nearly a quarter of a century could hardly speak of our loss, died in August 2001 at the age of eighty. Jim and Bill and I had gathered information for twenty-five years, cultivating friendships in the Defense Department and the State Department, and being kept up to date on the postwar interrogations of former POWs and Laotian citizens. There were reports of two Caucasians who had "become sick and died" while being taken to Northern Laos via North Vietnam.

The Joint Task Force for Full Accounting, a Hawaii-based military command in charge of repatriating American remains, had been hard at work all that time. We believed we knew where Charlie and Neil had been taken, and we believed that they had been executed on the way to North Vietnam.

The task force had miraculously identified a rice paddy four miles from the Vietnamese border which had been a battalion headquarters for a North Vietnamese construction unit during the war. I was welcome to come see what JTFA did in the field, and they would take me to the possible burial site.

In February of 2002 I went to Laos. When I flew into Vientiane, I spent a day getting briefed. Since I was still a sitting governor, visiting a country which almost never saw American dignitaries, the foreign ministry put on a mini-state dinner for me, complete with dancing and entertainment. They taught me the local folk dances. I knew as I was dancing that it was not unlikely that those entertaining me had had something to do with killing my brother. I walked around the city and down to the Mekong. Saffron-robed monks walked the streets, and there were small bungalows; maybe Charlie had stayed in one. Peaceful Buddhist music wafted out of run-down neighborhood temples along with the aroma of incense. The Lao were a lovely people. I knew why Charlie had come, and I knew why he had stayed, even with shells bursting at the edge of the city.

The next day the JTFA helicoptered me to their base near jagged mountains covered in green and sticking straight up out of the plain, mists rising from the valleys. The landscape was what I expected from the footage I had seen during and after the war, but it had never seemed real before. Underneath us peasants in conical hats scratched the earth the way they had for thousands of years. There were bomb craters everywhere, some right in the middle of villages. Laos, the colonel in charge told me, had been the most heavily bombed nation on earth during the U.S. bombing of the Ho Chi Minh trail. I believed it. Unexploded ordinance, including cluster bombs, still blow the hands and feet off Laotian children regularly, thirty years after the end of the war.

I had long admired the American military personnel; we were deeply grateful for their efforts to give us whatever information they had about my brother over all these years. The JTFA camp was filled with an all-volunteer force drawn from all four service branches, mostly career enlisted folks. They were warm people, coming from places like Detroit, Puerto Rico, and Texas, with stories about their families waiting for them all over America, all hoping, as was mine, that their mission was a success.

The JTFA took me to four dig sites, some on the sides of mountains where planes had crashed after being hit by enemy fire. A crash at 300 miles per hour pulverizes a plane on impact, and 25 years of scavenging in a desperately poor country leaves even less behind. To excavate a crash site, the JTFA hires entire villages to work under the supervision of an archeologist. The site is divided into grids, and workers dig until virgin soil is struck. The excavated soil is carried in buckets to a set of screens and sifted. I worked with the villagers, excavating and then sifting. The work was painstaking. Finding a tooth was cause for great celebration. Mostly it was tiny fragments of airplane parts and shreds of uniforms. Once in a while we'd find a tag or a ring.

On my last day in Laos, JTFA led me north to the border along a path similar to the one Charlie and Neil must have followed as they were taken to their deaths. They explained that they had reliable eye witness reports that the bodies of two American civilians had been seen in a bomb crater in late 1974. The trick was to find the remains in a three-acre paddy that had been graded heavily during road repair, and graded again when the North Vietnamese camp was turned into a rice paddy.

I asked to meet the witness, and the troops did not fail me. They introduced me to the farmer whose land would have to be dug up if we were to find Charlie and Neil, and to Mr. S., the witness. I gave them both gifts and thanked them profusely.

As we squished our way through the paddy, the Lao government minder, who went with me everywhere except at the base camp, somehow fell behind. Three of us, Mr. S., a young Thai-American soldier who spoke Lao, and I were left alone.

I learned that Mr. S. had seen the bodies and more. Neil had been thrown in the crater first, Charlie on top of him. Next to the crater was a shack which was full of fresh bullet holes. He thought the Vietnamese had either killed the boys or ordered the Lao to do it. It occurred to me that, given his age, Mr. S. might well have been involved in the executions.

As we piled into the chopper to return to Vientiane, I excused myself and ran back to the site alone. I stood at the edge of a small pond at the paddy and watched the water trickle through the terraces. It was incredibly peaceful, and although I thought it was pretty likely that the skeletons had been graded to bits long ago and scattered around the site, I knew two things: Charlie had loved Laos and the Laotian people, and if his remains could not be recovered, they had found a good eternal resting place. And I knew that I wanted to come back with my mother and my brothers. I also knew that the colonel, Kevin Smith, was a very determined person and that if anyone would make sure that the excavation would be done right, he would. I threw three American pennies I had bought from Vermont into the pond and went back to the helicopter.

When I got to the hotel, I went to my room and rang up $400 dollars worth of phone bills calling my mother, Jim, and Bill. Then I cried for long time.

Twenty-one months later, in the middle of my campaign for president, Jim, who had kept in very close touch with JTFA commanders and staff, got a call saying that they had found the remains. They were just as Mr. S. had said they would be, Charlie on top, facing up, Neil on bottom, facing down. JTFA cautioned us that they could not confirm their identities. But they described Charlie's unusual earth shoes, and the Vietnam-era POW bracelet he had worn since his days as a college student. The remains were to be repatriated the day before Thanksgiving.

A wonderful friend who was a campaign supporter made his plane available for a much reduced rate (we were legally required to pay something because of the McCain-Feingold Campaign Reform Act), and we flew to Hawaii for a very solemn ceremony. Ian Sharman, Neil's brother, had come from Australia, and in addition there were three other coffins that were unloaded from the belly of a huge C-130. I knew from experience that those other coffins probably contained little more than bone fragments and a few teeth.

The next morning we were allowed to see the remains. Both boys' skeletons were largely intact. Charlie's shoes, socks, and a pretty decayed but recognizable plaid shirt were with him. Ian recognized some of Neil's effects. There were also bullet fragments. They had been hit in the legs, the trunk, and the head.

Although we were cautioned that we would have to await further identification by dental records or DNA, we knew that the boys were almost home. We had our pictures taken with some of the troops and thanked them for what they had done for us and for what they were doing for hundreds of other American families like ours.

The fourteen-hour flight from Hawaii to Newark went quickly and quietly. It was a good quiet. Thanks to a lot of hard work by a lot of good people, we had closed the loop. A few months later we received word that the official identifications had been made by dental records we had sent to Hawaii long before. Charlie's remains were shipped east shortly after my last primary was over, and we buried the small white coffin in the same cemetery that was home to generations of his forefathers.

The road from Rosebud Farm had ended for one of the young men who wanted to make a difference. The others continue on their own roads, learning, growing, and teaching others. There is no life that is easy. Some lives are longer than others. It is, in the end, the quality that counts.

The sixties and seventies were times of great tumult in America. They were also times of exceptional progress, sometimes deeply resisted and deeply resented, even to this day. We are still fighting battles today over what went on 40 years ago. It is hard to believe that five years before Charlie and Neil were killed, many black Americans were barely allowed to vote. Birth control and abortion were illegal in almost every state. Most private clubs did not allow women or Jews to be members. A war was going on in which our own government systematically lied to its people. During the time the boys were in Australia, the President of the United States was exposed as someone who had covered up his knowledge of a burglary and used his power and that of the FBI to thwart any investigation into the Watergate break-in. That President, Richard M. Nixon, became the only one in history to resign.

For all those Americans who read this book but are too young to remember, the sixties and seventies were also a time of great hope and progress. Our generation believed in its government, was disappointed, and came back to hope again. The lessons and excesses of the sixties and early seventies gave way to the self-absorption of the eighties, the financial chicanery of the nineties, and the deceitfulness of the early new millennium. But the idealism of the young

Americans, those who went to Southeast Asia and those who didn't, has been toughened by the understanding that what they did mattered then, and matters now. American idealism will not be lost in this generation, and, in the next generation, will overcome fear once again.

—Howard Dean

AUTHOR'S NOTE

When my 22-year-old stepson was in Ghana, my husband and I heard nothing from him for three months except the two emails he sent when he made the long trek to Accra from the beach where he was camping. Only later did we learn that he had contracted malaria, became severely dehydrated, and had struggled through a slow and nightmare-plagued recovery until he was well enough to fly home. Relieved and grateful to see him in the spring, I thought of the dozens of young men I've heard about who have disappeared in wildernesses around the world—the wilds of Alaska, the jungles of South America, the mountains of the American West, rainforests of Southeast Asia. What is it that makes youths on the verge of manhood wander into danger? Does some siren song of independence draw them from the security and comfort of the familiar? Or is it that, like the Greeks Perseus and Theseus, they feel the need to prove their manhood by surviving a life-threatening quest?

There are pivotal times in our lives around which the rest of our existence turns. For many of us, that time was during the Vietnam era. Men were drafted or enlisted to fight in a war that hundreds of thousands of Americans opposed. Young people voiced their outrage through music, drugs, and alienation from parental conventions. "Tune in, turn on, drop out" was the mantra of the period. We dropped out of school, dropped out of society, and dropped out of the country. Of those who stepped outside their safety zone of private schools, junior country club memberships, privilege and prosperity, three found themselves on a farm commune in northern Australia, cultivating the unforgiving soil, butchering wild pigs, fishing in the Coral Sea, and shrugging off two decades of social training. Luxury gave way to practicality. They learned skills they had never dreamed of back in their ivy-covered ivory towers.

Most of the activists who protested the war, resisted the draft, questioned authority, and sought alternative lifestyles eventually would resign themselves to working within the system, go to graduate school, get jobs, raise families, and follow the examples of their parents. An exceptional few, especially those with the means to do so, would cling to the idealism of their youth and start their own traditions. The three Americans who founded Rosebud Farm in Far North Queensland—Kim Haskell, Rich Trapnell and Jeb Buck—turned away from their upbringing and committed themselves to a hard Australian life, one they are still living today. Dozens of friends visited the farm over the years. This story involves two who lived at Rosebud from 1973 to 1974. My husband, Harry Reynolds, would return to follow his dreams. Wanderlust would take Charlie Dean to Southeast Asia, where his life would end tragically.

For some young men, including the five in this book, it is not until they strip away everything they've known and discover life at its most raw that they can begin to live according to the morals and values they believe are truly their own. Some stand up to the tests they set for themselves; others, like Charlie, fall victim to their own ingenuous trust in human nature.

The Rosebud Farm project was born of idealism, commitment, and virtue, all deeply rooted in friendships that have transcended distance and time. The men in this story, insulated by wealth and innocent of heart, were trying to make sense of a tumultuous world and find some peace in it. And, in one way or another, they all accomplished what they set out to do. Through journals, letters, interviews and research, I have tried to piece together the months before Charlie's disappearance and his incarceration and execution at the hands of the Pathet Lao in the rainforests of Laos. Long reminiscences reaching back over thirty years to the untamed mountains and rivers of North Queensland and Rosebud Farm have helped me imagine the experiences of these young men.

CHAPTER 1

Laos, September 1974

The permanent temptation of life is to confuse dreams with reality.
The permanent defeat in life comes when dreams are surrendered to reality.

—James A. Michener
from Harry Reynolds's journal

The ferryboat sputtered down the Mekong, a high-pitched whir of cicadas challenging the drone of its engine. The wet season had just ended, and the banks along the Mekong River rose twenty feet above the silty water. Lush thickets brushed the shores of Thailand and rice paddies greened the hillsides of Laos. Crumbling shoreline barely held back the encroaching jungle, where locals believed every tree held a ghost. Pale trunks, gray and twisted, loomed forty feet above into a canopy that blocked the sun. In the distance, granite mountains ascended above verdant hills.

Charlie Dean, one hand on the camera looped around his neck, looked over the gunwale into the water, hoping to spot a catfish—some were reputed to weigh five hundred pounds. At the muddy water's edge, a woman stood knee-deep and dipped her laundry, clapped the red cloth between brown hands, dipped again. Nearby, children splashed and one boy urinated into the stream. A woman lowered a cup into the slow current, raised it to her lips and sipped. A water buffalo made his way to the river and dropped his head to drink. Charlie had read that the Mekong originates deep within the Tibetan Plateau and spills 2,600 miles south and east to the South China Sea. The checkered rice fields and tributaries that fed into the waterway were home to more than fifty million people. The river was their artery, their life's blood.

The air steamed and Charlie's shirt stuck to his suntanned back. He was three inches shy of six feet and drew his knees to his chest under the ferryboat's rickety cabin to make room for the other *farangs*—the Lao word for foreigner. The wooden hull was long and slender, the keel shallow to avoid bottom. While the *farangs* chattered and shifted position, a dozen Laotians sat absolutely still in the bow. When anyone moved, the boat rocked and changed course slightly. One mother curled her arm around a young boy and scanned the riverbank, watching. Every day she and her son remained in Laos put them in jeopardy. Although a peace treaty had been signed the previous year, civil war was still raging. The communist Pathet Lao, guided by North Vietnam, ordered village women to sew uniforms and took their children to serve as couriers. Men were snatched from the fields and sent to fight. Anyone who spoke out was shot. Charlie felt an unspoken tension in the boat, as if there would be serious consequences to pay if something went wrong.

His stomach was growing queasy from the engine's growling and exhaust fumes. He glanced at Neil, the Australian journalist Charlie had met in Darwin on his way to Thailand. Neil was just barely twenty-one, and it wasn't hard to convince him to take a leave from his newspaper job for a bit of sightseeing in Southeast Asia. The Aussie was a decent companion, a good bloke.

In a few more hours they were expected to arrive in Thakhek, where they would decide whether to move on to Nepal or head back to Australia. Charlie had mixed feelings about leaving Laos. He had spent the last six years speaking against America's actions in Southeast Asia, and during the past months in Australia his political vision had been hammered into a personal, spiritual fire. He knew he couldn't single-handedly settle the problems of these people whose lives had been so long tied up in warfare, but he could offer them the peace he carried in his heart. He had convinced himself that his sense of peace protected him from peril, even during his two weeks in the Khmer Republic where every night he heard the *wahump, wahump, wahump* of artillery being fired across the Mekong. Phnom Penh's sidewalks were crowded with Laotian refugees escaping the communists. The city streets, lined with trees and sidewalk cafes, were cluttered with sandbags, barbed wire, and American military supplies. Charlie had no doubt that the U.S. was still involved.

It was hard to believe that a land so beautiful could be torn by such strife. Charlie and Neil had climbed around limestone caves and swum through clear green pools into grottos covered with moss and ferns. Outside massive and exquisite temples, they watched monks glide in flowing orange robes through courtyards glittering with smiling Buddhas. Slim, slit-skirted women of Vientiane made them propositions. They ate croissants and drank strong French coffee in a decrepit café, its green walls smudged with dirt. Sitting in front of a whirling prop fan, they read the *Bangkok Post* while a lizard crawled across the ceiling.

When they had reached Paksan, a woman offered the two travelers mats on the floor of her one-room house.

Like most Laotians, she lived at subsistence level, eating only what she grew and could barter for in the village. She pointed to her mouth to ask if the young men were hungry, and Charlie nodded. He and Neil had not had much but *khao*—rice—since they left Bangkok several days earlier. While she went outside and lit the kerosene burner, the children watched the bearded strangers in scruffy clothing. Charlie rummaged in his pack. Inside was an envelope of candle-fruit nuts he planned to mail back to Rosebud Farm, where he had spent the last year. The fatty seed inside the shell was said to provide lamp oil, and Rosebud might be able to cultivate the tree. There was a letter from his brother Howard saying he had applied to medical school. Charlie was glad Howard had found his calling. In a pocket of the pack, he found a square of fabric that a Rosebud girl, Gayle, had embroidered and given him to sew onto his jeans. He had watched her fashion the paw-paw fruit, his favorite treat, at night by candlelight, making tiny French knots with black thread for the seeds. Even before she gave him the patch, he knew she was sweet on him. When he left, she made him swear to come back, and he had given his promise.

There were letters from Harry Reynolds and Kim Haskell, old boarding school friends with whom he had lived at Rosebud. Kim had founded Rosebud and had taught him to make commitments driven by passion, to live spontaneously and without apprehension, and it was those lessons that led him to Laos.

From the bowels of his pack Charlie unearthed his camera—a pricey single-lens reflex. He checked the film—still several shots left. Waving the children closer together, he framed them in the viewfinder and the girl and her brothers grinned for a couple of pictures.

The woman brought in two bowls of noodle soup with fish sauce, and the children sat quietly while the men ate. Charlie felt a stab of guilt and wondered if there would be enough for the youngsters that night. When the bowls were empty, the woman presented her opium pipe, offering a smoke. Charlie hoped she would not take offense when he declined her offer. She lit the pipe for herself. When he lay down, Charlie felt the mat soften as the sweet smoke settled over him. He thought how Laos was one of the least-developed countries on earth, and yet it had plenty of natural resources and a culture uncorrupted by capitalism. The people were gracious and kind. If Laos could resolve its conflicts, it stood a good chance of making something of itself. Charlie was twenty-four and roiling with ideas. He believed in basic human goodness—maybe he could find a way to help.

From the bow of the ferryboat, a lullaby—*Non saa laa*—sleep, my child, the mother sang. Charlie wondered about the children in Paksan, whether they would survive the civil war. The boys had reminded him of his own brothers. With any luck, he would be back home on Park Avenue by Christmas.

The boat drifted to the riverbank and stopped. Certainly they weren't in Thakhek yet.

Neil nudged Charlie. "Pathet Lao checkpoint," he said.

Several brown-skinned men motioned for the passengers to disembark, and Charlie was grateful for a chance to stretch his legs. The men were wearing Cooley caps shaped like wide cones, and each had a rifle strapped to his back. They looked like a gang of teenagers. When Charlie lifted the camera and snapped a picture, one of the men laid his hand on the barrel of the gun behind him. With the other hand, he reached for the camera.

Charlie had taken some shots of scenery along the Mekong, beautiful temples of Phnom Penh, the Paksan children. He had bought the camera in Japan, the first big expenditure of his life. The camera had kept a visual record of the two months he spent in Japan and the year he had lived at Rosebud Farm. He would not give up the camera.

"*Bo*," Charlie said and shook his head. "*Bo* camera."

The rifle suddenly swung from behind the man, rose to his shoulder, and pointed at Charlie's chest. The man was yelling, but Charlie had no idea what he was saying. He shoved Charlie, pushing him away from the boat and into the forest. Charlie twisted his neck and saw the passengers board the ferry again. The mother, hand on her son's back, went to the bow. As the boat left the shore, she looked at Charlie and mouthed the words *pai dee*—go in peace.

Neil stumbled behind Charlie, a cone-capped man gripping his arm. Charlie peered into the gloomy thicket in front of him and thought of the Laotian expression, "When the tiger sleeps, don't wake him." But it was too late—he had awakened the tiger.

CHAPTER 2

Senior Prefect

The mind is restless, turbulent strong and unyielding, as difficult to subdue as the wind.

—Bhagavad Gita
from the Rosebud Farm journal

Ten years before he found himself facing the forests of Laos, Charlie stood looking up at a chapel tower rising solid and imposing from a field of green, four spires pointing heavenward from each of its square corners. To the south, the cleaved cliff of Purgatory Rock ascended straight from the Atlantic Ocean. Gulls drifted by and waves lapped the shore. Footprints made by the bare feet of young men, some with surfboards tucked under arms, led over the sand and across the two-lane road, through a meadow and onto the groomed greens of St. George's School where Charlie was about to enter Second Form. He had not lived away from home before, home being Manhattan's Upper East Side in the winter and the Hamptons in the summer. But his brother Howard, sixteen months older, was a Fourth Former, and so St. George's was not new to him.

Charlie was ready to leave home. His father, Howard Brush Dean, was a strict disciplinarian who wielded powerful clout in his household. A political conservative, Mr. Dean made an impressive living as a top executive of Dean Witter Reynolds on Wall Street. Even so, he was fiscally vigilant. The four Dean boys were the only players on their Little League baseball team without the team uniform because Mr. Dean had refused to buy them uniforms they would just outgrow. Despite his small stature, Mr. Dean's friends called him "Big Howard" because of his blustery personality and raucous sense of humor. He once wrapped a dead cat in paper and ribbon and presented it to a friend as a birthday present. Such audacious acts made him both intimidating and the life of every party.

From an early age, Big Howard had taught his sons the virtues of nationalism and sacrifice for their country. During World War II he had worked for the China National Aviation Corp managing the transport of supplies for Chinese and U.S. forces in Asia, and he believed that serving one's country was a duty and a privilege, an honor that he expected would fall to his own boys one day. Husky-voiced, Big Howard led dinner-table debates on civic issues and demanded that his sons back up their opinions with hard facts. It wasn't enough to espouse a theory —they had to articulate a plan. Mr. Dean's political outlook was the final word at family gatherings, and only Charlie confronted his father's conservatism. On a visit home from boarding school, Charlie commented that LBJ was a good president. "I don't think you know what you're talking about," Big Howard told him. In the Dean household, only republicans were considered fit to govern. Charlie, hardheaded and refusing to be cowed, retorted, "Well, I don't think you know what *you* are talking about." The discussion ended in stony silence.

Big Howard raised his sons to be models of patriotism, virtue and breeding. On Sundays the family attended St. Luke's Episcopal Church in East Hampton. For their primary grades the boys were enrolled in the private Browning School on the Upper East Side. When they were ready for secondary school, the Deans looked for an environment that would season the boys morally and spiritually as well as academically. Big Howard considered Pomfret in Connecticut, his own alma mater, but when they visited the Pomfret campus, the students talked during Sunday chapel service and refused to stand and sing hymns. Big Howard was appalled at their disrespect and looked elsewhere. The Episcopal all-boys school in Newport, Rhode Island, met his criteria.

Manhattan and Long Island had prepared Charlie not to be intimidated by Newport's aura of wealth and power. Although in its early days Newport's harbors bustled with trade in rum, silver and slaves, by the mid-nineteenth century intellectuals and writers had claimed the colony as a summer retreat. Within a few years, industrial barons funneled millions of dollars into construction of stone and marble manors they called "cottages" in absurd understatement, mansions that still guard the coastline along the Cliff Walk in regalia of tended lawns and gardens. The lifestyle included elaborate dinner parties served by butlers in green and gold liveries. Newport had become a showcase and a sanctuary for the rich, who indulged themselves in opulence and luxury.

But the boarding school was sheltered from Newport's lavishness. St. George's founder, Episcopal minister John Diman, named the school after the martyred Christian soldier who saved a young princess from the jowls of a hungry dragon and slew the beast. Reverend Diman no doubt hoped such courage and integrity would leave its mark on

St. George's boys, and he situated the school two miles outside Newport on 230 acres of prime oceanfront property in Middletown, which the students dubbed "The Hilltop."

By the time Reverend Diman opened his doors to his first pupils, St. Paul's and St. Mark's were well established, but St. George's wasted no time in matching their stature. In 1958 the school was named to E. Digby Baltzell's list, *Select 16: The Most Socially Prestigious American Boarding Schools*. Baltzell, a University of Pennsylvania sociologist, is credited with originating the acronym WASP and made it his life's work to study and expound upon the behavior of the privileged. A prestigious boarding school, he wrote, had "the sociological function of differentiating the upper classes from the rest of the population." Charlie and most of his classmates fell within Baltzell's definition of the upper class.

St. George's asked its students to accept their social responsibility as members of the privileged. Charlie and the other boys would be groomed to be as successful as their fathers. To foster moral integrity, Charlie was expected to attend chapel services every day before dinner with an additional Sunday morning service and to wear a coat and tie both to chapel and to dinner. Trips into Newport were discouraged, and passes were limited to one a month. The 1968 *Lance* describes the attitude of the time: "Our expectations, like the green leaves on the trees in the soft light of a summer's fading afternoon, were high, were bright as our laundry fresh uniforms, as clear of fact as the open summer sky."

Astors and Vanderbilts had passed through the halls of St. George's School before the Dean brothers arrived. Howard, Charlie, Jim and Bill Dean in turn shared the company of other youth like themselves, who came from addresses like Greenwich, West Hartford, Oyster Bay, Nahant, and Old Lyme. The young men were taught to recognize their talents, to develop and hone them, and to do so with vigor. It was understood that they would spend their four years at St. George's readying themselves for good colleges and productive lives of service to the world and to God. Charlie took the St. George's charge seriously.

Like most of his classmates, Charlie brought his father's conventional world views with him to boarding school. He had stood behind his father when Big Howard supported Richard Nixon over democrat John F. Kennedy in the 1960 presidential election. But when Kennedy won the national election, Charlie saw attitudes begin to change.

In 1962 federal marshals escorted James Meredith to his class at the University of Mississippi in the first court-ordered integration. A year later, St. George's recruited the first black student, a local Newport boy, and gave him a scholarship for Third Form. But integration for its own sake yields disaster. The young man withdrew after his second year and was eventually arrested for beating his foster mother and setting fire to their home. At age 19, he committed suicide in prison.

Howard was already a school hero when Charlie came to St. George's. The older brother was a star on the football and track teams, captain of the wrestling team, president of the library committee, student council representative, dorm prefect, and all-around scholar. In the 1966 *Lance*, Howard described himself as "a solid conservative defending the powers of the Student Council and lashing out at cynics and opponents." His father had taught him well.

Where Howard had an angled chin and a hard set to his mouth, Charlie was more boyish looking. His cheek was smooth and there was a dimple in the generous chin. He kept his hair cropped above the ears, often tousled in sleepy neglect. He was born under the sign of Aries and, being a ram, was headstrong and tenacious. When Charlie set his sights, he would not be deterred. His eyes kindled with earnestness and integrity, as if he were ready to burst into a flame of good intention.

At SGS, Charlie followed Howard's lead and joined the choir, the school newspaper staff, and the Library Association. Devoutly religious, he was named head of the Acolyte's Guild and donned the ceremonial robes. Shoulders squared in the gravity of his office, he led the processions into chapel, carrying the staff bearing the cross. Charlie's spiritual ideals never wavered, even in his most trying times. Years later, when asked to describe Charlie, his brother Bill would note first Charlie's spirituality and second his dogged determination.

In sports Charlie was a participant but no athlete. His friend Harry Reynolds, a year behind Charlie, excelled as football quarterback while Charlie did his best as an offensive blocker. During hockey season, he sat the bench as back-up goalie while Harry scored most of the goals. On the baseball team, Charlie played outfield while Harry guarded first base and the dashing Kim Haskell, who was team captain, took to the mound as the star pitcher.

No hero on the playing fields, neither did Charlie excel in the classroom, graduating 49th out of 53 students in his class. Charlie's skill was with people. He was at the center of every school event, if not on the field, then leading cheers in the stands. The St. George's teams never had a more energetic supporter.

In his final year, Charlie's class elected him Senior Prefect—the equivalent to president of the student council— an honor which even Howard had not achieved. Under his senior portrait, a formal pose with blazer and St. George's tie, is written:

To talk about Charley [sic] Dean's merits as Senior Prefect is to belabor the obvious. His election bespeaks his popularity, his handling of the post to bring about more student privileges bespeaks his acuity, his rapport with both faculty and lower forms evidences his diplomacy, and his many extracurricular activities witness his multiplicity. We know he runs the Council in the Headmaster's study once a Sunday and walks the cross twice [as acolyte], but what does he do on his days of rest? He circulates, assimilates, manipulates.... He is as human and easy going as a Senior Prefect is allowed to be while still keeping the school out of dire peril.

Charlie handled his job as Senior Prefect with uncanny maturity. He made decisions about discipline with Headmaster Archer Harmon, determining whether a misbehaving student would be expelled or allowed to stay in school. He listened to his classmates, encouraging them to make use of the student council by voicing their complaints and suggestions, and he promised to bring to the headmaster the most feasible plan for correction or implementation.

No student concern was too small. Charlie was instrumental in having washing machines installed in the dorms, getting Saturday night privileges for seniors, and overseeing the St. George's Society and the Dining Room Committee to make sure they fulfilled their obligations to the student body. Although he was a procrastinator by nature, Charlie was confident in the governing seat. He had learned from his father how to express his ideas in the most convincing manner. Howard remembers Charlie's graduation dinner when, just before Charlie took the podium to address the guests, he sat scribbling on a piece of paper at the head table, looking anything but prepared. But when he stood up, he delivered an impressively polished talk with confidence and poise. Decades later, when Howard ran for U.S. President, he attempted to bring his brother's earnest spontaneity to the podium in his own speeches.

Although he was an ardent student leader, Charlie was far from a saint. When girls from the Wheeler School came for weekend dances, Charlie was among the boys who took their dates along the chapel's yellow tile path leading to the choir loft where they might grab a few intimate moments. The final full-page picture in the 1968 *Lance* shows Charlie and a classmate perched behind the captain's wheel aboard the St. George's yacht. The caption reads: "If it seems to you that the world has gone mad and nothing whatsoever can be done about it, try this for a start—." Each boy is holding an open can of Ballantine Ale.

Nine of Charlie's classmates matriculated at Harvard, and four others were accepted to Princeton, Yale or Stanford. His own board scores were impressive—higher than Howard's—and he was sure those and his participation in St. George's clubs would compensate for his low class rank. Nevertheless, every Ivy League college to which he applied rejected him. With no prospects for college, Charlie contemplated joining the Peace Corps, but Big Howard intervened. A few phone calls, and his second son was assured a space in the freshman class of the University of North Carolina at Chapel Hill.

In boarding schools, classmates become surrogate families. They arrange reunions and pledge themselves to lifetime partnerships. Teammate Harry Reynolds had been accepted to Harvard and Kim Haskell was bound for the University of Denver, but, whatever happened, the St. George's friends vowed to keep in touch.

As the last days of secondary school approached, several students received typewritten letters from SGS alumnus, Rhode Island Senator Claiborne Pell. "Graduation time, I know, is one of mixed emotions, a bittersweet experience of leaving high school behind," Pell wrote. "A way of life for you has ended and another has begun. The future ahead may not always be an easy one, but face it with courage and confidence in yourself. Your life will be in great part what you make it." Pell ended the letter by wishing "good health and a confident, cheerful spirit for your life ahead."

The "life ahead" was scripted for St. George's students by their families' desideratum, and they summoned courage for the trials they would face. They had sipped tea from china cups served from silver teapots. They knew proper attire, proper speech, and proper manners. The transformation from the malleable clay of young boys to the firm substance of manhood had come about through lessons in discipline, the trappings of privilege, and the bonds of friendship.

An inscription in the '68 *Lance* reads:

Cast out of the hatchery, and contemplating the tangled swampgrass of the outer world, we poise, on our own, rare and immaculate birds, half domesticated still, but filling with half-understood urges from our new exposure. We are awkward, but we'll grow to grace; we have only the vestigial skills for survival, but we'll develop a predatory eye and a spearlike thrust, iron stomachs and tireless wings, a compass in the mind and an hereditary wisdom for where the richnesses of the continent lie. Our lives will be a series of nests and migrations, heights, flights, arrowing flocks, and still waters.

Wings poised, Charlie and his fellow St. George's graduates were ready to take flight.

CHAPTER 3

Times A-Changing

Man should live nobly though he does not see any practical reason for it, simply because in the mysterious, inexplicable mixture of beauty, ugliness, virtue and baseness in which he finds himself, he must want to be on the side of the beautiful and the virtuous.

—Joseph Conrad
from Harry's journal

While Charlie had packed up and headed south for college, Harry retreated to the familiar scenery of Cambridge. The imposing columns of Widener Library and the stained glass windows of Memorial Church inspired a silent awe among many new students. Harry knew Harvard from his father and his grandfather, both Harvard men, and his great uncle, who was assistant to Crimson president Nathan Pusey. Harvard was in his genes and in his blood.

Harvard's tuition in 1969 was $1,760. Of the 1,200 students entering with Harry, 96 were African-American. Among his classmates were writer Al Franken, sports commentator James Brown, and Benazir Bhutto, who later served as prime minister of Pakistan. Enrollment included poor boys on scholarship and rich boys with pedigrees, like John Quincy Adams V, descendant of the U.S. President. Harry did not think about money or status, although he might have fallen somewhere in the middle in both areas. What he cared about was trying out for the hockey team.

He was appointed to Thayer Hall with roommates Webster Golinkin, a St. George's classmate, and Rich Trapnell, who had been senior prefect at Westminster School. Rich had been a boyhood friend of Kim Haskell, and, on Kim's advice, Harry had put Rich's name down as a roommate preference. Rich had a delicate handsomeness about him, the kind of unthreatening good looks that makes women feel comfortable. Although compact in size, he sparkled with wit and cheerfulness. Rich was interested in everything—politics, sports, campus activities—and he engaged his roommates in an easy comradeship. Rich's father worked for DuPont in Wilmington. A conservative who believed in a firm national defense, Mr. Trapnell disapproved of the company's move from manufacture of gunpowder to plastics. Nevertheless, DuPont gave him a good living. A bigger disappointment was his son's decision to attend Harvard instead of the University of Virginia, his own alma mater, and for an entire summer he refused to eat with Rich at the dinner table. Even though Rich and his father had serious differences on nearly everything, for graduation from Westminster Mr. Trapnell presented Rich with a brand new 1969 Oldsmobile 442 convertible—forest green with beige interior. It had cost $4,100, a staggering sum.

Harry, Rich and Web shared a two-bedroom suite— Harry in the double with Web and Rich in the single, separated by a large common area. The three had similar enough backgrounds to be at ease with each other and different enough personalities to keep things interesting. Their days were taken up with classes and extra-curricular activities.

Harry made the freshman hockey team, Web got involved in drama, and Rich took up the big bass drum emblazoned with a red H and marched in half-time formations during Harvard football games; yet when they came together back in the rooms, they were friends. Rich got them all tickets to see Sly and the Family Stone, and Sly's "I'm gonna take you higher" became a theme for the roommates. Harry called Rich "Buster," Rich shortened Webster to "Weebs," and the three cruised around Cambridge in the Olds, top down, singing the Beatles song "We all live in a yellow submarine" at the top of their voices. They gave each other confidence and support for coping with the rigors of college life during what Rich refers to as "an incredible place and time."

On autumn afternoons, the voices of Crosby, Stills and Nash, James Taylor, and Bob Dylan wafted from open dormitory windows and across Harvard Yard on wisps of marijuana smoke. "The times, they are a-changing," Dylan sang. Hair grew shaggy, and whiskers appeared soft and fuzzy on nearly every chin. Button-down-collars and three-piece suits attended classes with black turtlenecks and jeans. Walking to meals, students of kindred attitudes and styles stuck together like schools of fish, not game to venture outside their circles. Rich remembers the energy in Harvard Yard as extraordinary—"So many minds collected in the one place. It was truly electric, frightening, and totally exhilarating."

The world seemed to turn faster in those days. The young men had watched on TV as Apollo 11 landed on the moon and had been hypnotized when Neil Armstrong and Buzz Aldrin took the first steps on moon dust. As they were packing for college, half a million people converged on Bethel, New York, for the Woodstock music festival, and they had missed the counterculture carnival of drugs, nudity, free spirits and free love. Harry's favorite TV program was The Dick VanDyke Show, and he had a boyish crush on

Mary Tyler Moore. Although they didn't have much time for television, they occasionally caught episodes of Gunsmoke, Laugh-In, and the Red Skelton show. If they were even vaguely aware of the eighteen Americans who within the previous four years had committed suicide in opposition to the War in Vietnam, eight by setting themselves afire, the deaths seemed remote and unconnected to their own lives.

The spring before the three roommates arrived in Cambridge, Harvard students had taken over University Hall to voice their objection to the war. As a result, the college disallowed the presence of ROTC on campus. Neither Harry nor Rich was interested in ROTC—hockey gave Harry enough discipline. Since his father had been a military man, Web might have considered it, but ROTC meant commuting to the M.I.T. campus, for which he could not spare the time. Mostly they were occupied with the Olympian task of passing their classes. Even so, Harry felt obliged to do his part for the anti-war effort. He wouldn't have wanted to be a soldier, and he couldn't see that communism was an immediate threat to his own way of life. He didn't understand why America couldn't just get out of Southeast Asia and let them fight their own battles. So, one or two afternoons a week he took the subway downtown and handed out flyers against the fighting and then caught the train back to Harvard in time for hockey practice.

Rich had been following the escalation of the war more closely and heard that the Student Mobilization Committee, along with the Young Socialist Alliance, was planning a massive rally for October 15. Harvard was renowned for its open-mindedness and for offering a forum for debate, and bowing to that propensity faculty voted overwhelming support for the rally. Ninety percent of instructors canceled classes that day, giving Rich leave to attend the rally.

Along Commonwealth Avenue, banners bearing the peace insignia draped from windows. People leaned over sills. Students from Northeastern, M.I.T. and Boston University as well as Harvard clad themselves with black armbands, carried anti-war posters and sang protest songs— "Blowing in the Wind" and "Give Peace a Chance." Rich estimated the crowd at Boston Common to be near a hundred thousand. Senator George McGovern told the group: "Let's stop saving face and begin saving lives." Ministers, political science professors, welfare workers and a member of the Socialist Workers' Party all spoke, warning that they were tired of rhetoric about ending the war. If anything, the fighting was gaining momentum. The call was for action.

Rich's impression was that America was fighting two wars—one in Vietnam and one at home. The war at home was multi-sided—kids against parents, students against schools, protesters against the war, radicals against the government, and blacks struggling for their freedom. He felt the crowd swelling with indignation and believed a massive upheaval was taking form, and he knew he'd be swept up in it.

When the demonstration ended, the Student Mobilization Committee declared the rally a success and a building stone for the march on Washington to be held in November. Rich planned to drive the Olds to the Nation's Capital; he wouldn't miss the action. For Harry, peace rallies were not an option. With the sole exception of Christmas Day, hockey required him to be on the ice every afternoon from October to March, no exceptions.

At St. George's School, Harry had been more speed than stature, and his teammates called him "Squeak." But now he stood just over six feet and weighed nearly two hundred pounds. By nature he was practical and efficient, and he whittled his wardrobe down to bare essentials—khakis, sport coat and tie for traveling to away games, and for non-game days a one-piece white jumpsuit that zippered up the front, the type worn by garage mechanics. In the mornings, he zipped the jumpsuit over boxers and tee shirt for class, and there was no fumbling with buttons when he changed for hockey practice. On chilly days he donned a sweater over the jumpsuit, and when winter set in, he added a jacket. Harry's sartorial minimalism helped him deal with the bedlam building around him.

For Rich, the November march on Washington had ignited a fuse. When fifteen thousand gathered at Government Center in February to protest the jury's decision in the trial of the Chicago Seven, he was among them. He had only heard about the riots during the 1968 Democratic National Convention in Chicago, but he was infuriated by Judge Julius Hoffman's ordering defendant Bobby Seale bound and gagged for insisting that his constitutional rights had been violated.

Harry was not with Rich at Government Center that day. He was battling Cornell in the ECAC hockey semifinals, a contest Harvard would lose while the Cornell team went on to win the title. When the season ended just as spring break began, Harry flew to Vail for some skiing with his old friend Kim Haskell. In the evenings they watched the news detailing President Nixon's new Vietnamization plan, originally designed as a gradual withdrawal of American troops from Vietnam and a transfer of military duties to the South Vietnamese. But when the North Vietnamese Communists stepped up their attacks and used supply lines in Laos and Cambodia to equip and feed their troops, Nixon increased bombing in Laos and ordered U.S. forces to invade Cambodia.

The United States had been fighting in Southeast Asia for three years and nine months. It looked as if America was in the war for the long haul. At first all that meant for the friends was more of the protesting that had become part of college life. So they mixed a few cocktails in their rented condo and toasted each other on their good fortune not to be involved in the pandemonium. Then came Nixon's announcement that the government planned to draft by lottery 150,000 American men over eighteen. Each day of the year was printed on a piece of paper, and the papers were placed in blue plastic capsules and deposited in a large glass jar. The capsules were drawn from the jar, one by one. The first date selected, September 14, was given the number one, the second date, April 24, was assigned number two, and so on, until each birth date had a coinciding number.

Harry said if he were drafted, he guessed he'd have to go although he couldn't imagine shooting at anyone, even the Viet Cong. Kim swore he'd leave the country before he'd go to Vietnam. Within the next year, over 170,000 young men would declare themselves conscientious objectors. Others would burn their draft cards, chanting "Hell, no, we won't go," and over a hundred thousand would flee the country—tens of thousands to Canada and others to Sweden and Mexico. Barry Bondus of Big Lake, Minnesota, broke into his local draft board and dumped two buckets of human feces over its records. Catholic priests Phil and Daniel Berrigan poured pig's blood over the records of the Cantonsville, Maryland, draft board. Over three thousand went to jail for refusing induction.

Both Kim and Rich drew numbers over two hundred, which put them out of danger of being drafted. Charlie Dean's birthday was one of the last to be drawn from the jar, and he too was safe. Harry's assignment was number 181, and shortly after the drawing his orders came to report for his physical.

He had heard stories about ducking induction, including paying a psychiatrist to write a letter to the draft board saying the patient suffered from anxiety, wet himself, curled into the fetal position under stress, or had homosexual tendencies. One man, just before his physical, inserted a fish into his rectum, tail fin hanging out. Another cut off his ring finger. Depending on the leniency of the draft boards, many creative dissenters were released from their obligations. But Harry thought of his father, who had served in the Marines. His father would want him to do what was right.

At the Boston headquarters, Harry stripped down to his boxers and waited, nearly naked and trembling at the prospect of going to war. Because of his hockey workouts, he'd never been in better physical shape. Other than a geology class he had failed because he'd slept in instead of going on the required field trip, his grades were pretty good—good enough, he hoped, to keep the army from carting him out of school. Not surprisingly, he passed the physical, but his student status held. He could take to the ice his sophomore year with a deferment and a colossal sense of relief.

The draft lottery provoked more anti-war action, most of it on college campuses. Students wore shirts silk-screened with red fists, threw bricks through shop windows, looted, and bombarded police cars with beer bottles. Harry had grown up on Boston's cloistered North Shore, and nothing had prepared him for this indignation, this violence. His long-time friend Sam Burr, also a Harvard freshman that year, had been assigned a room in Massachusetts House with an ROTC roommate. Sam's windows overlooked Harvard Square and Massachusetts Avenue, and Harry, Web and Rich gathered in Sam's room to watch the rampage from a safe distance. The hostilities tangled them all in personal conflict. Although Web opposed the Vietnam War, he had grown up with deference for the military. Harry's father had left Harvard to fight in World War II. The administrations of their parents' era had been honorable and fair. To get involved in the riots would go against everything they had been taught to believe, yet to stand by and watch felt traitorous. But Nixon was asking young Americans to pay for his mistakes with their lives, a sacrifice they were not willing to make.

Although they kept their distance from the chaos in the streets and held a tight rein on their emotions, it was hard to focus on their studies. The Boston Globe was filled with stories about campus protests that spilled into downtown areas with students waving placards reading "No more napalm" and "Shame on America" and setting fires in the streets. As they cried out for peace, Civil Defense Unit officers flogged them with billy clubs and bullied them onto buses in mass arrests.

As Harvard students were reviewing for final exams, the radio blared news from Kent, Ohio. There had been a rally at Kent State College that had gotten out of hand, and police threw tear gas canisters to disperse the crowds. Students retaliated by pelting officers with rocks, and troopers responded by opening fire—67 shots in 13 seconds that left four students dead and nine wounded.

Rich was outraged. "It was like a bad dream gone wrong and going and going and going," he remembers.

Harry, Rich and Web joined other Harvard students packed into Memorial Hall, all of them upset and confused. The deaths of the Kent State students made the war personal. They voted to strike and walked out of classes with other Harvard and Radcliffe students. Harry and Rich wandered around campus that night and found groups of students up at the Cliffe, talking about what was happening in America, what they could do about it and whether the war would ever end. They had thought their demonstrations would make a difference, but now the world seemed to be coming down around their ears.

The Harvard administration supported the strike and closed the campus, giving students midterm grades as finals.

There was a full eclipse of the sun that spring. At the instant of the total coverage, the freshmen surrounding Harvard Yard opened their dorm room windows, pointed their speakers into the Yard, and set their record player needles down on George Harrison's song, "Here Comes the Sun." At the darkest moment of the eclipse, a hundred recordings of the song started, each a millisecond out of time with the others. So it was with students all over the country—all tuned to the same melody, each playing it her or his own way.

As the St. George's yearbook philosophized, children of privilege have an in-bred wisdom for finding "richnesses of the continent" and a determination to seek out the best for themselves. That seeking would take the friends in very different directions. Rich went back to Delaware and Web to New York. Harry got a job in Wenham delivering dry cleaning and tried to save a few bucks. On his days off, he tied his surfboard to the roof of the delivery truck and drove to the shore to catch some waves. For that summer Massachusetts gave him respite from the nation's insanity.

CHAPTER 4

Outward Bound

like a fruit uneaten
i await consummation.
the end
is the beginning.
the journey in, the breaking out.

—from the Rosebud Farm journal

K im Haskell learned from an early age not to accept limitations. His grandfather, vice president of DuPont and in charge of production during WWI, taught him that obstacles were only challenges, and challenges were to be met with intellect and courage. His father, known to his friends as Hal, had served in WWII as an officer and in 1953 was hired as assistant to Nelson Rockefeller at the Department of Health, Education and Welfare in Washington. When Rockefeller became a cabinet member to advise the President on new foreign policy initiatives, Haskell went to the White House with him. A taste of politics made him salivate for public office, and when President Eisenhower won re-election in 1956, Haskell was elected to a term in Congress, taking the lead in modernizing air traffic control and creating the first student loan program. In the late fifties, Haskell acquired control of Abercrombie & Fitch, at the time a sporting clothier, and as CEO catapulted the company into the realm of the young and hip. While Kim was heading off to boarding school, his father was back in Delaware being sworn in as mayor of Wilmington.

Described by a friend as a far-reaching man with great vision, Hal Haskell appeared inexhaustible, and so did his bank account. To say that the Haskells had money hardly gave a picture of the extent of their wealth. They kept homes in Florida, South Carolina, Maine and Delaware and a farm in Chadds Ford, Pennsylvania, where Hal ran a dairy business. The stone farmhouse at Chadds Ford is adorned with original paintings by Andrew Wyeth, a friend of the Haskells. At the Boca Grande house in Florida, Hal kept a deep sea fishing boat.

Kim, the first of Hal's eight children, cut his teeth on a big game fishing rod. Christened Malcolm Wells Haskell at birth, Kim was not snobbish about his father's money. He emanated charisma. At Fay School in Massachusetts, where he boarded for seventh and eighth grades, he was picked as student leader to the disciplinary committee and helped decide who would be punished for rule viola-tions. He watched the brawny master deliver the penalty with a leather strap to the buttocks, the boy either crying or accepting the whipping defiantly. The beatings soured Kim toward authority, and he became the first Fay School student body president to resign his office.

By the time he enrolled in St. George's School, Kim was primed for rebellion. He stole out after curfew, smoked pot, drank beer, and sneaked girls into his dorm room. A cool-looking boy with black hair longer than prep school authorities liked, he slipped under the wire and took risks without getting caught. The masters knew about his exploits, but he was smart enough not to leave a trail. In the 1969 *Lance*, Kim writes of himself: "Fourth Form meant a lot of time to break rules and no time for work." His only appearance in the yearbook for his junior year is a candid shot taken in the library, dressed in a jacket and tie with an unidentified girl on his lap. He channeled his energies into baseball, and when he wasn't catching, his formidable knuckleball was the terror of SGS rivals. Secondary school was the highlight of Kim's formal education. The friends he made there, including Harry Reynolds and the Dean boys, would be for life.

During the summers of 1967 and 1968, Kim honed his leadership skills by working as an intern in the U.S. Senate with J. Caleb Boggs of Delaware and took an Outward Bound course to learn wilderness survival, both of which would be more useful within the coming years than he could imagine.

At the University of Denver, Kim spent his freshman year plodding along, changing his focus from business to English, and going through the motions of being a student. That spring, rattled by the Kent State shootings, Denver students set up Woodstock West, a barricade where Kim and some of his classmates watched for National Guard troops who might be planning to storm the campus to quell student unrest. Kim's room was on the tenth floor of his dorm, overlooking the hockey rink across a parking lot. At five o'clock one morning after he had been up all night cramming for exams, he looked out the window at headlights—lots of them—lined up in the parking lot. Twelve hundred uniformed National Guard troops, called out by Governor Love, assembled at dawn with fixed bayonets on their rifles, mobilizing to march through campus. That morning marked the last day of Kim's formal schooling, and he walked away from campus for good.

The following summer, Kim sat on the front porch of the Chadds Ford house with his father.

"You're wasting your money sending me back to Denver," Kim told him.

"What do you want to do instead?" his father asked.

Kim wanted to explore a world bigger than the boundaries of the United States.

"I want to go to Africa," he said.

Hal knew better than to try to coerce his oldest son into doing something against his will. He had raised his sons and daughters to speak their minds.

"Why don't you go to Africa, then?" Hal said.

"I don't have any money."

"How much do you need?"

"Five thousand would do it."

"Bullshit," Hal told him. "Come on down to the office tomorrow and I'll write you a check for $5,000, and we'll see how far you get."

Kim called up Rich and Wilmington chum Chris Patterson, who had just finished his first year at the University of Pennsylvania, and convinced them to come to Kenya with him. "We couldn't fight for a lost cause or remain in a land where we totally disagreed with all present authority," Kim said, "so we left to find a life where we could make decisions and choices, the way we wanted to and the way that felt right to us."

Although Kenya was in the midst of its own political turmoil, the three friends found enough distractions to keep them out of harm's way. Rich wrote to Harry from a safari in Nairobe:

Africa is so out of sight…. The animals here are unbelievable. Today we filmed a leopard killing a hare. I'm using my 'rents 16 mm Bell & Howell—it sucks, but we've filmed rhino, cape buffalo, elephant, lions (we've seen 47 so far), gazelle, giraffe, hippo, and other assorted weird animals and birds…. Haskell and I are having a ball. Seriously—it's really good.

With land at five dollars an acre and the government welcoming immigrants, the trio was tempted to stay in Africa, but short on cash and with no job prospects, they returned home. The political atmosphere in the States had not improved in the six weeks they had been gone. The war in Vietnam was still raging and turmoil dominated the civil rights movement. Chris went back to Penn, but Rich had missed the deadline for re-enrolling at Harvard. Neither Rich nor Kim wanted to live at home. Kim's father was such a public figure that "If Kim brushed his teeth the wrong way, it got into the newspapers," according to Rich. It didn't take them long to realize they'd been better off in Kenya.

Before they made a decision about the next move, Rich and Kim drove to Washington and walked into Senator Boggs's office to voice their protest against the Vietnam War. The senator listened patiently and agreed to do what he could. In the meantime, he said he had a nephew living in Sydney, and if they were thinking about traveling, they might try Australia. Both Kim and Rich agreed that Australia sounded like a fine idea.

They made a quick trip to Cambridge, found Harry, and spent a couple of days trying to talk him into loading into Rich's Oldsmobile and heading with them at least as far as California. Persuasive as his friends were, Harry was primed for the upcoming hockey season. He had made the varsity team, and his skates were steadfast to the ice.

Without Harry, Rich and Kim gassed up the Olds, put the top down, and started across the country. When they reached Eureka, they toasted each other with Mateus wine and pot. In their celebratory mood, Rich plowed the Olds into a fence. He found someone to pound out the dents, drove to Stanford, and sold the still practically new car for $1,400. That and what Kim had salvaged from his father's five grand gave them enough to buy two one-way tickets to Sydney with plenty left over for whatever adventure they could find.

CHAPTER 5

The Buck Nixon Club

We are sharing a time which is unexplainable.

—from the Rosebud Farm journal

For the past few summers, Charlie had volunteered as a counselor at Boys Harbor, a camp near East Hampton that gave a hundred disadvantaged kids from Harlem, Bedford Stuyvesant and Hell's Kitchen a chance to spend a month in the country. Half were African-American, a third Latino, and the rest a mixture of ethnicities. One of the goals of Boys Harbor was to help the campers learn to compete academically with their more privileged peers. The work taught Charlie patience, tolerance, and skill in dealing with people, all qualities he would call into use in the next few years.

When Charlie entered the University of North Carolina at Chapel Hill in the fall of 1968, Richard Nixon was embroiled in the presidential campaign against former vice president Hubert Humphrey. Charlie, fresh from St. George's School and eager to be involved in campus politics, joined the Young Republicans Club and threw his support behind Nixon. His efforts were mostly symbolic; the age of eligibility would not be lowered to eighteen for three more years, when Congress would pass the 26th Amendment.

The third floor of Hinton James dorm housed a sprinkling of students from New York, New Jersey and Connecticut, but the majority were native North Carolinians. The local boys referred to the northerners as Yankees, and the northerners responded in good humor with nicknames for the southerners—Don Wright from Goldsboro was dubbed "Dyno-Don" after a popular drag racer from New Jersey.

From the start, Charlie gained the trust of both groups and they elected him representative to the student council. Declaring a political science major, he launched himself into campus government, entering into dialogue and debate on every issue from international relations to the nuances of UNC life. As he had at St. George's, Charlie advocated for his classmates and introduced a resolution calling for an end to the campus curfew for women and a bill to replace aging ice machines in the dormitories. When it came to Nixon's Vietnam strategies, Charlie began to realize that he had been funneled into a narrow channel instead of thinking on his own. This war was not winding down, as Nixon had promised. If anything, the fighting was intensifying.

Disgusted with Nixon's lies, Charlie switched his allegiance to the Democratic Party. With his political evolution came a transformation in his appearance. He grew his hair to chin length, cultivated a neatly-trimmed beard, and replaced his khakis with bell-bottom jeans. He no longer had any use for the blazer and neckties from his St. George's days. The glint of innocence in his eyes transformed to a burning mission to right the wrongs he saw in the world. For the moment, his spiritual and political affinities were aligned. One of his major initiatives was sponsoring the April 1970 Environmental Teach-In, which became known as the first Earth Day, a resolution delegating some student fees toward fighting world hunger.

During Charlie's freshman year, members of the Black Student Movement organized a strike of dining hall workers to demand higher wages for the university's cafeteria employees. Students carped when they couldn't get a good meal on campus and demanded that the administration do something. Worried that their resentment would turn violent, the governor ordered the North Carolina National Guard to stand by. In late March the strike ended in a compromise, but students began to realize their power.

While UNC-Chapel Hill was thought to be the liberal bastion of the South, most of its students were from conservative southern families and less inclined than those on northern campuses to dissent. But in the fall of Charlie's sophomore year, a group of students gathered on the UNC-Chapel Hill greens to protest Nixon's failure to withdraw from Vietnam. After graduate teaching assistants staged a strike, activism became part of campus life.

Charlie committed himself to campus peace efforts. He and classmates Gerry Cohen and Elizabeth Anania (now the wife of former North Carolina Senator John Edwards) organized campus peace rallies and anti-Nixon demonstrations. As with everything he undertook, Charlie threw himself into action with his whole heart. Cohen says that Charlie had "a bulldog personality"—once he bit on an issue, he would not let go. And for Charlie, the Vietnam War was all-consuming.

When the school year ended, Charlie moved out of Hinton James and into a decaying, unheated frame house on Merritt Mill Road in Carrboro with new friends Peter Caron from St. Mark's School, Peter's brother John, a couple other prep school northerners, and a few dogs. Railroad tracks ran through the inauspicious front yard, and behind the house stood a concrete factory. The tin-roofed structure had a front porch, two small bedrooms, one painted red and green and the other purple and yellow, and a larger bedroom where Peter slept. The five shared one barely functioning bathroom. In the living room, they painted three of the walls each a different color, and the fourth wall they spattered with leftover paint for a Jackson Pollock effect. The landlady, a tolerant black woman named Bessie, requested a total of fifty dollars a month in rent, which she apologetically raised to sixty dollars during the winter when she added central heat. It was usually Charlie or Peter who delivered the rent check to Bessie's house. She had two pictures on the wall of her living room—one of President Kennedy and the other of Jesus—and fed the boys slices of sweet potato pie each time they came. The accommodations offered them a short walk to campus and a sense of liberation.

Beer, pot and music were the main components of Merritt Mill culture. Songs blasted constantly from the windows and doors—Grateful Dead, Rolling Stones, Grand Funk Railroad, Quicksilver, Derek and the Dominos. Peter had spent a year in London after boarding school and had gotten to know the British rock groups, which he introduced to Merritt Mill long before they hit it big in the U.S. Three pennies taped to the stereo's tone arm kept the records from skipping while they hosted parties with dancing on the bowed and trembling floorboards. Everyone came to Merritt Mill—heads as well as jocks. Ike Ogelsby, the star quarterback on the football team in 1970, fell off the front porch and broke his hand. The accident sat him on the bench for the rest of the year and foiled the Tarheels' hopes for a winning season.

As they had at Hinton James, the Merritt Mill residents looked to Charlie for leadership. Charlie was captivated by Karen Ellis, a theater major with deep dimples and an impish grin, and on the spur of the moment he invited her to Carrboro for dinner. When the housemates learned there would be an extra mouth to feed, they panicked that there might not be enough food to go around and began picking bloody, half-cooked chicken pieces from the barbecue grill in a feeding frenzy. Charlie said little, but his disapproving look was enough. The chicken found its way back to the grill, and twenty minutes later the group sat down to a civilized meal. "What sanity was there," Karen recalls, "Charlie brought into it."

Merritt Mill became a gathering place for students and a parade of visitors to talk about politics and plan strategies for making their views public. They believed they were in the right, and they were absolutely sure they could convince the government that peace was more effective than warfare. Articulate and outspoken, Charlie held forth on issues with the fervor of his father. But there was little question that Charlie would break from the Deans' four-generation tradition of Wall Street businessmen, leaving that responsibility to one of his quieter brothers. Devilishly handsome in his new whiskers, he had replaced the acolyte's staff with the banner of student activism.

Howard had taken a year off for some work experience and was just a year ahead of Charlie when he returned to Yale. On his occasional visits to Carrboro, he took over breakfast duties as chief flapjack flipper and after graduation lived at the house for two weeks while he planned a trip to South America. During those days Howard talked with the housemates about Charlie Reich, one of his Yale professors and author of the book *Greening of America*. Reich, who padded barefoot to his classes, condemned the American economic system as materialistic and so strictly conforming to a traditional hierarchy that it crushed individuality and free expression. Reich lauded hippies for their desire to make technology work for humanity and the sense of personal freedom to "do their own thing." Advocating less cement, more trees and parks, and a slower, simpler lifestyle, Reich called for rage against the Corporate State, which he saw as a mindless automaton running roughshod over humanity. Charlie, who had just turned twenty-one, listened to his older brother and took notes.

For their twenty-first birthdays, Big Howard gave Howard and Charlie each twenty-five thousand dollars and enough cash to buy a used vehicle. Howard invested in a reliable sedan. Charlie had borrowed his roommate Don's car and totaled it, leaving him with back pain that would trouble him for the next few years. When his birthday rolled around in April, Charlie used his father's gift to buy a large gray school bus equipped with makeshift kitchen and toilet. The Merritt Mill boys christened the vehicle "Omnibus" and took their first road trip to the Dean's East Hampton house. Mr. Dean was in the city at the time or he would have bristled as Charlie ignored decorum and escorted the hirsute group into the elite Maidstone Country Club as his guests for a round of lawn tennis.

That summer Charlie and a few of his Chapel Hill friends planned to drive Omnibus to Colorado, where they hoped to get jobs at Loveland Pass and make a few bucks. The bus got them as far as Spartanburg before the radiator gave out and they had to have it replaced. Five miles outside Golden, Colorado, the engine blew and they managed to push Omnibus into a gas station. Two local boys offered to fix up the bus for a case of beer. Late at night the locals appeared with a working engine and hooked it up to the Omnibus frame. The Chapel Hill boys asked no questions, but they suspected the engine had been stolen. They handed over the beer, glad to be on their way again.

The parks at Loveland Pass required union membership, so the dreams of making money were dashed. Instead,

Charlie suggested they head to California, where they ran a free transport service up the Coastal Highway, picking up hitchhikers and dropping them off as they worked their way north. In Berkeley they met up with Howard, who joined the group for hiking in Yosemite National Park. The bus's second engine turned out to be little better than the first, and gallon jugs of water were kept filled to make sure the engine didn't overheat. The drive up Donner Pass in Sierra Nevada, an elevation of over seventy-two hundred feet, taxed Omnibus to its limit. Every ten minutes Charlie stopped the bus along the ascent to add water to the radiator. The landscape was stark, dry and hot, and the boys were tired, grumpy, and in desperate need of showers. At the wheel, Charlie felt his frustration growing as the engine gasped for relief. Finally, he pulled the bus over, sat by the roadside, and buried his face in his arms. For Howard, it was the closest he had ever seen Charlie to giving up. He encouraged Charlie to board the bus again, and in a few days the gray Omnibus and its fragrant passengers crossed the George Washington Bridge into New York City.

When Charlie graduated from UNC, Nixon was refueling for a second term in office. Charlie was rabid about unseating Nixon and signed on as chair of the campus campaign of democratic nominee George McGovern. McGovern was one of the first liberal Democrats to oppose American involvement in Vietnam. "I loathe the war in Southeast Asia," McGovern declared in a campaign speech, "and if I become the President of the United States, that war would end, and I mean that with all my heart." Karen, who volunteered to be the campaign's finance chair, said Charlie was almost pathologically dedicated to the cause. To show his dedication, Charlie, the only paid staffer, quietly endorsed all his paychecks back to the campaign.

Charlie's distrust of Nixon's political tactics proved well founded when on the night of June 16 a group of inept burglars broke into the Democratic National Committee's headquarters. Investigators followed a trail of evidence that led to the Committee to Re-Elect the President. Journalists Bob Woodward and Carl Bernstein of *The Washington Post* launched an in-depth investigation into the burglary, ultimately reporting that Nixon had authorized the FBI to cover up the scandal.

Nixon's corruption enraged Charlie, and he intensified his efforts on McGovern's campaign. One of his initiatives was the Buck Nixon Club, whose motto was "Buck Nixon before he bucks you." He had buttons printed up bearing the logo "Buck Nixon (I Did!) McGovern '72" and gave them to students who pledged one dollar (a buck) a week for the nine weeks of the campaign. The motto's crude innuendo most likely had something to do with the success of the drive. Student volunteers raised thousands of dollars by going door-to-door in the dorms, collecting single dollar bills. Charlie recruited Chapel Hill High School students to travel around the state on weekends, canvassing for McGovern. Down to the wire, he organized a Labor Day rally in the Great Hall at the Carolina Student Union, where North Carolina AFL-CIO President Wilbur Hobby gave a robust speech in support of McGovern. Following Hobby's talk with his own, Charlie roused the crowd, promising that McGovern would carry North Carolina.

But McGovern did not take North Carolina. In fact, Nixon won all states except Massachusetts and the District of Columbia. In his concession speech, McGovern was gallant. "If we pushed the day of peace just one day closer," he said, "then every minute and every hour and every bone-crushing effort in this campaign was worth the entire sacrifice."

Charlie was devastated by McGovern's loss. He wrote to Karen that he had "crashed from a dynamite trip...like being hit by a landslide." Even in his despair at McGovern's defeat, Charlie thought to thank her for helping to preserve his sanity during the campaign. "By the time you came in in the afternoons," he wrote, "I was really ready to hear about dance class or the latest romance at Playmakers," the student theater group. Karen had been Charlie's confidante, his friend, his lover. For her, Charlie was everything she admired in a man—intelligence, integrity, and a passion to make the world better. Before he left Chapel Hill, she gave him a POW bracelet, which he would wear for the rest of his life.

When the Dean family gathered in New York for Christmas, Charlie wrote Karen that he was thinking about "getting back in there" to "keep fighting." The problem was that he didn't know what battlefield to enter. Howard urged him to travel—if he saw some of the world, he might get his perspective back. Charlie knew he had to find his New Jerusalem—his inner destiny and a state of spiritual peace. In March, he caught a ride to Seattle and boarded a freighter heading for Japan. His old teammate Kim Haskell had written him from Australia, urging him to come. Maybe he'd wander down there eventually. Maybe somewhere on the other side of the globe he would find some sanctuary.

CHAPTER 6

Wallaby Roadkill

Australia is leaping after the U.S.—hopefully there will be enough heads to make some changes before it gets as fucked as us.

—from a letter to Harry from Rich in Darwin
March, 1971

When Kim and Rich reached Sydney, they called Senator Boggs's nephew, who gave them space on the floor of his flat while they got themselves acclimated to the southern hemisphere. For $600, they bought a VW Kombi Ute, a vehicle half van and half pick-up, and found someone to weld a frame across the back so they could fasten on a tarp for camping. Kim named the van "Big Mama" and equipped her with two spearguns, a .22 rifle, a shotgun, a two-burner propane stove, cooking gear, mattresses, and fishing rods.

Big Mama, it turned out, ran on youthful will and excessive amounts of oil. Two hundred miles west of Sydney they stopped in Warrnambool, the van leaking too much oil to continue without a repair. There was nothing to do but find a pub and wait for the mechanic to work some magic. It was Christmas Eve and as presents to themselves they shouted each other to hot two-dollar meals and forty-cent bottles of brew.

Pubs are social centers in small Australian towns, especially around holidays. Two Aussies, looking scrawny and road-weary, bought them a round of beers, and Kim reciprocated with another round. The young strangers were living for the moment in an old Australian army tent in the middle of a caravan park and invited the two Americans to share the space. If a man did not get exactly what he wanted from the world, then he would take what the world delivered to him and take it with gratitude. The tent's floor was commodious enough to spread out four sleeping bags, and so the Americans and their new friends passed Christmas without elaborate ado.

One of the two Australians, a teenager who called himself Jap, had not been much farther than Sydney. He was skinny, unemployed, homeless, broke and ready for anything. Kim and Rich figured a native would make for good company, and Jap and his meager pack boarded the repaired van for the trek toward Adelaide and then, with any luck, Perth.

The road across the Nullarbor Plain started with three hundred miles of dirt track and deteriorated into two thousand miles of absolute desert without a tree in sight— just low saltbush and bluebush scrub. It was summer, and temperatures reached 110 degrees during the day and dipped into the low nineties at night. They took turns driving and sleeping, putting as much sand behind them as the old van would tolerate. Most of the cars had metal grates welded over their grills to protect them from night collisions with kangaroos. Red kangaroos can grow to six and a half feet tall and leap at forty miles an hour through a car's headlamps. Wallabies are smaller and not quite so swift, and several times driving in the dark Kim swerved to avoid a marsupial of one variety or another. The morning dawned on hundreds of wallaby and kangaroo carcasses along the road. When they took a break outside Perth, Jap skinned and gutted a freshly killed wallaby, and they roasted it over a hastily constructed campfire. Although kangaroo meat was usually used for dog food, Rich declared it palatable.

They talked about the Vietnam War, although Jap knew little about Australia's role in Southeast Asia. He had heard that Australia was involved, but he had no way of knowing that more than 59,000 Australians would serve in Vietnam during the period of the war nor that over five hundred Australians would give up their lives in the conflict. Australians were mostly opposed to the war with groups of anarchists, pacifists and libertarians organizing anti-war marches. Australia had a conscription program similar to the draft lottery in the United States, and many young men went to jail rather than being drafted. Others opted for an alternative civilian work program if they qualified as conscientious objectors, which required simply declaring oneself religiously or morally opposed to the war. In any event, Jap figured if the government wanted to enlist him as a soldier, they'd have to find him first, no small task along the vast stretches of desert.

When they finally reached Perth, they found elaborate architecture and an impressive coastline, and the boys thought they might get jobs and stay awhile. For the right price, Rich and Kim were willing to do blue-collar labor, but there were few offerings, especially for Yanks. So they found a garage to service the van and then headed out for Darwin on a humbling three-thousand-mile drive along the dustiest excuse for a road they had ever seen.

Along the coast, Kim was seduced by the ocean. Water held enchantment over him. He liked the way the sun rose from the horizon in the east and sizzled itself out on the western horizon. He matched his moods with the tides and his breathing with the billows. The waves clapping onto shore called to him, and he was useless until he had satisfied his longing to answer. With snorkel, mask and speargun, he was at home in the sea's belly, matching wits with fish and ray and octopus and snatching from rock cavities crayfish as big as lobsters. Once he wrestled a sea turtle into submission, which made for an enormous feast. When he speared a trophy, he brought it to the sand and pierced its brain with a spike so it wouldn't suffer. For Kim, the highest honor he could pay his prey was assimilation with a little salt and pepper over an open fire.

The shore was desolate and empty, and the men shed their clothes in the heat and swam to keep cool. When they encountered a rare human, they scrambled for clothing and generated stares for their long hair held out of their faces with Indian-style headbands. On rare occasions they booked into a caravan park and ran their salt-encrusted bodies under a freshwater shower.

What towns that existed along the road north were no more than work camps for the iron ore and salt mines and, in many cases, just strings of tents and caravans. Kim reckoned that they were much like the old West towns of the U.S. a hundred years ago. They applied for jobs in a salt mine at a hundred dollars a week, more for the experience than for the money, but the foreman was looking for permanent help, not scraggly-looking transients.

After an eternity of driving, they reached Darwin, capital of the Northern Territory and busy port city for exports of cattle and oil to Southeast Asia. Darwin bustled with vitality, and the three men were ready for some urban distractions. Kim's Wilmington friend Jeb Buck dropped out of Princeton and worked his way to Darwin on a freighter. Jeb was good looking, a musician and a craftsman, and he added an aesthetic element to the company.

The four found an apartment and split the cost three ways, giving the penniless Jap a rent scholarship. Jeb was attracted to Darwin's local theatre group and landed a part in a play, and Kim oiled up his boarding school knuckleball and earned a pitching position on a local baseball team. "The pitchers throw about three-quarter speed, right down the old pipe," Kim wrote to Harry. "When I chucked a few knuckleballs around, the people here went berserk." He added that Harry would have an easy time playing semi-professional hockey in Darwin. "They even asked Trapnell and I to play, so that shows you how bush their league is," Kim wrote.

Kim was always cooking up schemes for himself and his comrades. He fired off letters to Delaware friends and St. George's classmates, painting Australia as a young man's Mecca and urging them to come. He wanted them involved in plotting out his latest idea, a venture making educational films in Africa. In the meantime, he hoped to break away from Darwin before the Australian winter set in and move on to Queensland, where he had heard, he wrote to Harry, "the mushrooms and grass grow wild."

CHAPTER 7

Treading Water

I sometimes look into the past for some set of memories out of which to make myself a story, but there are none in which I can recognize myself, none that can contain my overflowing life. I realize then that I only live in each fresh succeeding moment.

—Andre Gide
from Harry's journal

Harry had not heard from Charlie Dean his entire four years at Harvard. He assumed Charlie had graduated from college and gone on to some worthy endeavor. In the meantime, Harry focused on his game. He was big and fast, and he skated with grit and muscle. In the last year, he had grown another inch, put on five more pounds, and become a formidable forward on the ice. By the final season, he had gone through four pairs of skates and well over a hundred sticks. On game days, he ate training meals with the team of steak, pancakes and eggs. After games, they hung out at one of the campus clubs, playing pool and joking around together. They were like a family that demands of its members their undivided attention.

In boarding school the masters had kept close guard on students, especially during dances and other social gatherings, but at Harvard such parietals were considered anachronistic. Sex and nudity were celebrations of the spirit, and no one worried about STDs. Harvard rattled the Apollonian rituals of undergraduate life by allowing Radcliffe women to live in three of their dorms, but Harry was too intimidated by Cliffies to ask one for a date. Although strikingly handsome, a gap between his front teeth made him self-conscious, and he scrunched his shoulders to look smaller so that he wouldn't tower over women. Cliffies seemed always ready for intellectual sparring, and any man gutsy or naïve enough to debate them over the issue of gender politics would lose. Charlie might have stood up against them, but Harry was no debater and he would rather have faced off with a Boston Bruin than meet a Radcliffe woman in a verbal contest. In some ways, his coaches—Cooney Weiland and Bill Cleary—had shielded him both from the women's liberation movement and the antiwar and civil rights commotion during his years at Harvard. Had he not had the focus of two hours at the rink every day—and the exhaustion that followed—he might have been caught up in the lunacy and maybe have drifted away to Australia with Rich and Kim. But hockey held him suspended in a cocoon of training, practices and games so that every thought and action was wrapped around pucks, sticks, blades, nets and ice.

Of course, there were parties, but very different from the ones Charlie was hosting down in Chapel Hill. Clubs at Harvard were similar to fraternities, and Harry pledged the Owl Club because a few of the other initiates were sons of his father's friends. As with all Harvard clubs, membership was exclusively men. The Owl Club was housed in a noble old mansion graced with leather chairs and couches and had an aura of gentlemanly privilege. While young men studied, watched television and mingled, the club's steward, a fatherly old Irishman, made deluxe sandwiches for lunch and kept the kitchen well stocked. The pool room lent itself to soft-spoken recreation, and the mahogany-mantled fireplaces spoke of respectability. Those not raised with the accouterments of social and economic advantage soon acclimated. Those used to privilege expected no less.

Harry's favorite professor was John Kenneth Galbraith, one of the most renowned economists in America. Standing at an impressive six feet eleven inches tall, he filled a room. The course was based on Galbraith's book, *The New Industrial State*, which emphasized the importance of national fiscal planning. In manufacturing a product, Galbraith said, one must have foresight of what actions will be required and at the same time make preparations to accomplish those actions. Harry took the advice personally. He needed foresight, and he needed a plan of action.

The summer before his senior year, he bought a 1968 Dodge Dart for $180, in the trunk of which he found an expensive set of golf clubs—right-handed, though, so they were of little use to him. He sold the clubs and used the car to commute from Wenham to his job as a waiter at the Casablanca bar. The bar was owned by an enterprising Dutchman known as Van, a handsome, charming fellow with a European accent and a licentious sense of humor. He once bragged that he could entice a woman, lure her to an upstairs room, seduce her, and be back down at the bar within seven minutes, a feat that Harry, who had had little success with women, found most impressive.

Casablanca was on Brattle Street at the end of a long subterranean hall. Bogart and Bergman stared wistfully from wall murals in classic scenes from the movie. The club was a regular hangout of Harvard types, and Van commissioned an upstairs space for a dance floor with good music. The bar's reputation grew, and locals from the seamy sections of Boston started coming to dance. Van had no objection to one or two students of color, but he worried about an invasion of non-students from Roxbury and Dorchester. So far they stayed mostly on the dance floor, but he was afraid their presence would change the atmosphere of Casablanca. His solution was to turn the bar into a club, and he handed out crimson cards to hand-selected patrons—all of whom were white. In jocular spirits, the card read:

> *Member assures that He or She is not a pimp, whore, hustler, huckster, dope addict, dope peddler, purse snatcher or any other variety of undesirable asshole. Male member assures that he will not molest or otherwise disturb female members who indicate their desire to be left alone.... PAX VOBISCUM.*

To get a card, one showed up at the door for Van's inspection and, in most cases, Van dealt out a pass. Black applicants were turned away. Most of those rebuffed did not go peacefully. Van stood firm against curses, threats, righteous anger, and promises that he had not seen the last of them. Mostly Harry waited tables, but once in a while he spelled Van at the door. At those times, when he rejected people Van considered undesirable, Harry felt the impact of the new policy. Since the antiwar protests, blacks had become more vocal about asserting their rights. The African-American population in the Boston area was large in number and an intimidating presence. They did not take well to their exclusion from the club, and they did not give up knocking at the door. Van's discrimination would be his ruin.

Harry waited at the bar one evening for the bartender to fill an order so he could deliver the drinks to a table. At the door ten feet away, Van argued with a black man. Van was shaking his head, hands up as if to push the man away. Harry heard a loud pop, and Van fell back onto the floor. A bullet from a pistol fired at point-blank range had gone into his chest and through his heart. Harry stood a moment, not willing to believe what he had seen. He thought it odd how little blood there was. How odd, too, to see his employer, a man he knew well and admired, lying dead at his feet. Not just dead, but killed. And his killer was running down the hallway toward the door, making a getaway. Suddenly havoc broke loose, people screamed, and someone called for an ambulance. But the ambulance would arrive too late.

Later, Harry would think about Van's death, about how little he felt when Van died. Was that what Vietnam was like, with fellow infantrymen dying at a soldier's side? Did the soldier feel anything except relief that the Vietcong bullet had whizzed past him and found another target, just as he had been relieved that it was Van at the door and not himself? Was life really so ephemeral that a man could be hale and hearty one minute and lie lifeless the next? If that was fate, then, as far as Harry was concerned, fate had no conscience.

The Casablanca was closed until after Van's funeral. When it opened again under new ownership, the club status was dissolved and the dance floor eliminated. Harry didn't go back to work there that summer—it was time to get ready for his final season of Harvard hockey. Other than his car and a 1965 BMW motorcycle, he had few possessions and even fewer prospects for what to do with himself after graduation. His sister Kathy had graduated from Boston's Pine Manor College but stayed in the area with her fiancé, David Chandler. They bought season tickets to Harvard home games and usually invited Kathy's best friend Marjorie. Afterward, they met Harry at the field house for the traditional post-game reception.

A year older than Harry, Marjorie was tall and blonde, bubbly and talkative, and she loved being in crowds of people. Harry was dazzled by her. She had just broken up with a law student, a smooth, handsome fellow who had shattered her heart, and she was looking for some first-aid. Harry offered her balm. He started taking her to the Casablanca for a drink after a game, and sometimes they went to parties at the Pieta Club, whose members were athletes known for their wild revelry. The clubhouse was like a smoky bar— beer kegs, a sticky floor, and Saturday night strippers hired to dance on the pool table. The initiation to Pieta involved drinking lots of beer from one of the club's bountiful kegs, taking off one's clothes and, library card in hand, dashing naked into Widener and bringing back a book stamped by the desk clerk. When Harry undertook his initiation, an amused student on desk duty stamped his book, but he was sufficiently inebriated so that he has no memory of the title of the volume he retrieved.

Eventually Marjorie took him to her Cambridge apartment for the night, and in the morning he went back to the dorm for breakfast and a day of classes. The winter and spring of his last year at Harvard were occupied with hockey, studying, parties, and Marjorie.

Graduation hung like a precipice at the end of a long highway. Always self-critical, Harry knew he could have done better at Harvard, both academically and athletically. His diploma would say *cum laude*, but with more effort he might have added magna. If he had worked harder, he might have moved up from third to second line on the team. He might have scored more goals. He could even have had an offer to turn pro. An agent had shown some interest and he had considered the proposition, but he didn't want to ride the bench, which is probably where he would have ended up most games on the pro circuit. He'd had plenty of rewards for his successes over the years and had gotten satisfaction from games he had played well, but there had been just as many frustrations. He was ready to take a break from the ice. "I'm coming to the end of one stage in my life which has been comparatively easy and sheltered," he wrote in his journal. "Everything is not going to be so mapped out in the future." Until now, the next step had always been planned for him. When he set his foot down after Harvard, he had no idea if it would find solid ground.

By the beginning of Harry's last semester, the United States had reached a fragile peace with Southeast Asia. In January President Nixon gave his "Peace with Honor" broadcast, declaring a cease fire and promising that "all Americans held prisoners of war throughout Indochina will be released [and] there will be the fullest possible accounting for all of those who are missing in action." He did not elaborate on how he would fulfill that promise. From what Harry had read, some of the prisons were hidden so deep in the jungles that not even a bloodhound could find them, and he suspected that Nixon was perpetrating another one of his lies to appease an irate public. Nevertheless, the peace treaty was to be signed in Paris by Henry Kissinger, head of National Security Affairs, and Le Duc Tho, special adviser to the North Vietnamese delegation. In truth, South Vietnam President Nguyen Van Thieu had agreed to the treaty reluctantly, calling it "tantamount to surrender." The treaty would be flimsy at best.

Harvard's yearbook *Three-Thirty-Seven* declared that the war was over. "Now, it is no longer The War, as it has been for so many years.... Now it is simply another war, receding into the past, leaving behind it a legacy of pain and hatred." Campus politics had cooled, and students were talking about working within the system. Most had moved on from the protest music of the past three years and now listened to jazz. Harry's favorite album was *Swiss Movement* by Les McCann and Eddie Harris, peppy piano and percussion with an upbeat bass and an adroit sax. Instead of angry lyrics, Les McCann turned his political oppositions into musical art. Harry liked the spontaneity of the improvisation, the liveliness of the rhythms and the intelligence of the riffs, and he listened to the album over and over.

Harvard President Nathan Pusey called for Harvard men to serve the world of reason, modesty, charity and trust, even in the midst of deceit and anger. Web Golinkin was serving by entering the business world back home in New York. Two of Harry's Winthrop roommates were going on to medical school. Sam Burr had another year at Harvard, having taken time off to study rhesus macaque monkeys on an island off the coast of Puerto Rico, and then he planned to go into farming. Harry wondered what his old school-mate Charlie Dean was up to.

While he figured out his next step, Harry took a bartending course and got job behind the bar at the Casablanca, where he drew drafts and uncorked bottles, mixed daiquiris and Harvey Wallbangers. He worked hard and avoided small talk, traits that came naturally for him.

Now that he was living back in Wenham, he saw Marjorie only once or twice a week. He had hoped to push the relationship forward—not marriage yet, but definitely a commitment of some sort. But she was making noises about moving to New York and studying to be a paralegal, and he had no intention of living in a big city. Wall Street finances did not interest him, nor did graduate school—at least not yet. With Marjorie's looks and charisma, he realized glumly, she'd probably find someone in New York more her type.

While Harry treaded water, letters arrived from Australia urging him to come to Queensland. Australia was a paradise for young men from the East Coast, Rich had written. Unemployment was practically nonexistent, women outnumbered men in the cities, Americans were still heroes from World War II, and the landscape was an open campground.

Harry began to think seriously about going to Australia. He knew his parents wanted him to get a job in a bank or go to business school. But every year of his life had been occupied with school and hockey. He wanted people to know he was more than just a hockey player. He needed time to think—and to do that, he needed to get away.

When Harry confronted his father with his decision to go to Australia, his father nodded and puffed on his pipe. Phil Reynolds had a gentle nature and believed in letting his six children make their own decisions—and learn from their mistakes. About Harry's plans, he had only two questions. When would he be back? Harry wasn't sure, but in order to get the round-trip fare, he had to book a return. He chose the end of February, understanding that his stay might be extended—or, if Australia turned out to be a disillusionment, he would fly back earlier. Phil's second question was what would he do when he returned? For that Harry had no answer.

On August 25, Marjorie drove him to Logan Airport. The parting was bittersweet. Harry would miss her, of course, but he had never felt worthy of her. "I think she was expecting me to be greater than I actually am. I've fooled myself into thinking I deserve someone as great as Marj," he wrote in his journal. But he took comfort in the prospect of seeing his old classmates again. Motorcycle and hockey equipment stored in his parents' garage, he took a deep breath and boarded the United Airlines jet for Sydney.

CHAPTER 8

Sundowners

A beginning is a time for taking the most delicate care that the balances are correct.

—*Dune*
from the Rosebud farm journal

While Charlie and Harry were dealing with their own challenges, Kim and Rich kept their promise to explore Queensland. It has been said of Queensland that it is beautiful one day, perfect the next. Aussies call it the Sunshine Coast and book their vacations along its beaches. But Rich and Kim were drawn farther inland, to the farmland of Kuranda. For the Djabugai aborigine tribe, the name Kuranda means "meeting place of the spirits." In this ancient terrain, the mossy mountains of the tablelands rise one behind the other, all the way to the horizon, and the Barron River carves graceful curves through the rain forests. Settled at the highest end of the Barron Gorge, 1,080 feet above sea level, Kuranda is verdant and tropical. Vegetation flourishes in the lush atmosphere, and in the early seventies, the woodlands looked as untouched as they must have over a hundred million years earlier.

Of the 460 acres for sale just outside the village, two-thirds were thickly forested and too rocky and hilly to farm. Scrub brush blemished the arable land, but Kim saw promise. He thought he might even be able to do something with the wooden structures that looked as if they'd seen better days, and he plunked down the seventeen thousand dollars his father had sent him to buy the workable 160 acres, which included a house, a cattle yard, two permanent creeks and two tractors, only one of which was in working order. Following Kim's lead, Rich and Jeb bought the remaining three hundred acres, and the expatriate compound was underway.

In 1890, the land had been cleared for a coffee plantation, and a farmhouse was built. Thirty years later, the farmhouse had been replaced with a simple, three-room bungalow. By the time the boys took over, the wood plank walls and exposed ceiling beams were still standing. They had met a talented young Australian named Garry Wayne, who volunteered to mastermind the construction of a bunkhouse in exchange for room and board. "The house has a room with seventeen bunks built in—for lots of wommin!" Rich wrote to Harry, his familiar cheerfulness shining through the page. Hauling the building materials up the precipitous Kuranda range from Cairns proved too much for Big Mama, and the van was laid to rest. The bunkhouse was finished nevertheless and accommodated the Aussie entourage Rich and Kim had accumulated—Jap, Garry Wayne and his girl-friend Heather, Sneakers, Colin, and Colin's seven-year-old daughter Clare—with plenty of room for guests.

One of the guests was an American friend named Hutch. He had seen the movie *Citizen Kane*, where news-paperman Charles Kane's dying utterance was the word "Rosebud," the name of his childhood sled. As a boy, nothing had given Kane more joy than sliding down a hill in the snow, and the name Rosebud had come to be associated with youthful pleasures. Enthralled with the farm project, Hutch declared, "This is my Rosebud." The name stuck. Sneakers painted a flower on the front door and scrolled the words "Rosebud Farm."

Rich talked a neighboring farmer into using his tractor to plow up a half acre, and he set to planting potatoes, pumpkins and melons. There was a gardener in him. He understood the need for a seed to sprout and grow and produce, to fulfill whatever potential called to it. He liked the fierce, quiet life that showed itself in the fruit of the trees and the beauty of their flowers. "On the road to Cairns there are three huge orange orchards and in the last few days the blossoms have come alive—the aroma is so nice!" he wrote. He hoped to plant citrus trees—orange, mandarin, and grapefruit.

Water was the first order of business. The boys dammed a stream running not too far from the fields, and the reservoir served as irrigation source, bathing pool and drinking water, which was carted to the bunkhouse in buckets. Web Golinkin had turned Kim on to the *Dune* series, Frank Herbert's futuristic tales set on the desert planet Arrakis. In the book, wealth is measured in water, the supply of which diminishes each day, and water is so scarce that spitting is a sign of reverence. Arrakis was a desert planet whose leaders balanced politics and economics with conservation—a good model for Rosebud. The farmers would have to learn to appreciate what water they had and be grateful for a stream that didn't evaporate in the dry season.

In a town as small as Kuranda, with a church, a general store and two pubs—Top Pub at the high end of Main Street and Bottom Pub at the lower—news about the Rosebud Farm undertaking traveled fast. Any initial suspicions locals had for the nonconforming "freaks" turned to curiosity and then admiration for the way the enterprising young

Yanks had taken a neglected piece of property, cultivated it, and coaxed fruit trees to prosper. Their produce became the pride of markets in Cairns. The inquisitive stopped by the farm regularly, and backpackers found their way to Rosebud almost every day. Rich called most of the transients "sundowners" because they arrived at sunset, saying, "We've heard of this place—can you show us around?" It would be too late to move on, and they would be grateful for a meal and a cot. Some stayed a week, others a month, and one woman hung around for five years.

In the bunkhouse—which Rich christened "The Wompin' Room"—no less than a dozen bodies at a time camped out. Cooking took place in the smallest of the three compartments, but farm residents had no room to sit down together. Something had to be done to ease the crowding.

The Americans had come from families where obstacles were met head-on and resources were called upon to solve problems. So it was with the sons at Rosebud Farm. No one ever said, "We can't do this"; the question was "How can we do this?" Garry Wayne had grown up on a sheep and cattle station in far western Queensland and had done an apprenticeship as a boilermaker welder. He had learned carpentry from his father and there was nothing related to farming or building that he couldn't handle. Jeb was creative with woodwork and had the money to purchase the materials. The two sketched out a gathering house to accommodate the growing society. The building would have a meeting room large enough for playing music and dancing and an eating area for which Jeb would build a community-size table. The kitchen would have a wood cook stove and plenty of shelves for supplies, and a covered verandah would overlook the gardens. Jeb purchased two truckloads of timber at $2,500 a load, enough for the basic building. An old hotel next to one of the Kuranda pubs was slated for demolition, and he and Garry Wayne took the farm truck and scavenged timber and rosewood posts for the expansive front deck.

Jeb dubbed the structure The Top House. Solid and aesthetically pleasing, it backed against a hill, the front lawn bowing to a sunset view. The engineering was primitive, but the building was large and sound. Built-in couches lined the living space, which they called "the parlour," and the dining table seated twenty-four along its benches. After dark, candles and kerosene lamps shined homey light, and the battery-powered tape player gushed one of seven hundred cassette tapes in the Rosebud collection. Pink Floyd, Stevie Wonder, Dylan, Jethro Tull, and the Doors crooned into the tropical air. Jeb moved in a piano for evening jams and fingered mellow melodies. When he took up the mandolin, Rich tinkled piano chords and Sneakers plunked his banjo. Kim played the flute, sweet as sunrise birdsong. From the kitchen came the percussive clatter of pots—twang rump thump—and the thud thud of naked feet on floorboards, twirling skin squeaking on wood and bodies glowing golden with sweat and moonlight. Music, singing and dancing swirled around the fruit trees and field vegetables late into the sultry nights.

Around the Top House table, in front of one of Heather's meals, the farmers debated agricultural issues. One discussion involved the possible purchase of an island in the Coral Sea in partnership with the commune at Cape Tribulation, near Cooktown. Kim was pleased with the way Rosebud was developing, but the farm was seventeen miles inland from Cairns and a half-hour drive to the shore, and Kim wanted a closer connection to water. His father had sailed yawls in Bermuda and the Annapolis-to-Newport races, and Kim had learned to bait his fishing line and dangle it off his father's game boat before he could put a sentence together. Kim absolutely had to find a way to be near the sea.

The Cape Tribulation men had told him about Houghton Island, a one-square mile coral atoll that was on the market. Thirty-five miles north of Lizard Island and ten miles off the coast of North Queensland, the island was available for a thirty-three-year lease. Cape Trib, as the commune was known, offered to split the cost of $650 a year each. The deal sounded good, and a gang from Rosebud agreed to go out and have a look.

Tully Falls, a sixty-foot tugboat run by friends of the Cape Trib group, was heading out in mid-December to deliver bee hives and fruit trees to settlers on the coast at Temple Bay, and they agreed to drop the campers on Houghton Island. The boat would be back within a week to pick them up. Kim and Rich boarded the tug with Jap, Garry Wayne, a fourteen-year-old from Cape Trib named Jimmy, and two American visitors, Tom Blagden, a Harvard classmate of Rich's, and his girlfriend Lynn Scott. Lynn had grown up with Rich and Kim in Delaware and had enticed Tom into coming with her to see what the boys were doing on the other side of the world. They had been at Rosebud less than a week when the Houghton Island proposition came up. Tom brought his camera and several rolls of film to shoot pictures of tropical wildlife, and he looked forward to an authentic Australian adventure.

The group packed a tarp, fishing gear, generous bags of rice, and a 44-gallon drum of water, enough to last ten days. Jimmy contributed a hefty stash of Cape Trip marijuana. Along with the gear, they took a fourteen-foot aluminum boat with a tiny engine and just enough gasoline for a few days of fishing.

Whether it was the unkempt condition of the Tully Falls or the fact that each day for the past three weeks the tugboat captain had told them, "We're leaving tomorrow," Kim was nagged by some misgivings. He had a feeling the tugboat crew couldn't be counted on and loaded in an extra drum of fresh water, just in case. When they neared the atoll, the Rosebud contingent piled into the dinghy and putted to the Houghton Island beach.

Kim could see at once that the island was a disappointment—nothing but broken coral, driftwood and spear-leafed sisal plants. The few coconut palms were barren of fruit, and there were no freshwater streams or springs. He would need to bring in building supplies and have water tanks shipped in and set up. Farming was out of the question on the coral atoll without huge rainwater tanks or a desalinater, and the sandy reef held little promise for anything other than beach lounging and fishing. But the fishing was outstanding. Kim, Garry Wayne and Rich speared cod, coral trout, mangrove jacks and crays. Tom threw his line from the boat and reeled in trevally and permit. The campfire meals, fit for royalty, were followed by a smoke and an unrestricted view of the sunset.

The eight watched the sea change color as the sun made its way across the cloudless sky, turquoise turning indigo at the horizon. They swam and fished, napped and sunbathed, and indulged in the drinking water.

Toward the end of the week, Rich started to worry about the seedlings and the vegetable fields, and Tom and Lynn were itching for a fresh-water shower. Kim scanned the horizon for the rescue tugboat. No sign. They agreed to ration water—no water for washing, and no more than four cups a day for each person for drinking, an amount dangerously inadequate for surviving on a dry island in tropical heat. But the eight stuck to the limits. The Australians regarded Kim and Rich as the authorities, whether it was because of their educated intelligence or their apparently endless financial resources. Tom and Lynn didn't argue, either. Kim seemed to have an innate sense of survival, even in such an unforgiving landscape.

Eight days passed. Nine. Ten. The dinghy's 1.5 horsepower outboard faltered. Since they were down to the last gallon of gas, Kim suggested that they conserve the fuel and fish from shore or with snorkel and spearguns while they waited for the Tully Falls to arrive. They marched the circle that defined the island like hands on a slow-moving clock and watched the water for signs of the tugboat. Someone had brought binoculars, and in the distance they could see freighters in the deep sea channel four miles off. None would venture off course far enough to spot the stranded company and even if they did, a freighter wouldn't endanger its hull by getting close enough for a rescue in the shallow waters along the reef.

No one acknowledged the passing of Christmas Day. They tried digging a well with a camp shovel, but finding potable water on an atoll was hopeless. In the shadeless heat, the Rosebud crew discarded their clothes. Naked, unbathed and wild-haired, they might have been living Golding's *Lord of the Flies*. Even so, these young adults regarded each other with courtesy and civility. It would have been easy to blame Kim for their predicament, but they'd all come of their own free will. How could any of them—even Kim—have expected to be forgotten?

After two weeks, the fishing lines were stripped and most of the lures lost. They were down to two spearguns, and Kim, Rich and Garry Wayne juggled harpoons to try to feed the stranded company. They fished themselves into exhaustion and caught barely enough for one meal a day. It was the wet season, and Kim had counted on trapping rain to supplement drinking water, but never once did a water-bearing cloud come near the island. As the third week drew on, the jug's water level dwindled to dribblings. They had enough to last one more day—maybe two—before the situation grew desperate.

Images of family members came to them. They saw visions of death and the crazed hallucinations of dehydration. They slept and dreamed of stout ships and tall drinks. Kim remembered *Dune* during those hours. He might have spat reverently had he not wanted to preserve every drop of moisture within his skin. He thought of nomads who wandered the deserts of Arabia and aborigines who walked the outback of Australia, and he focused every atom of his will on finding a way out of this predicament.

While the young humans struggled with near delirium, birds went about their business of bringing clams to the island and harvesting the meat from their shells. Sea turtles nosed the shore. In the middle of the Great Barrier Reef the sea teemed with life, but their own existence was delicate and tenuous. How ironic, they must have thought, that they should perish on the island while life went on around them. What kept them calm was the spiritual balance of nature's energies and an unreasonable faith in miracles.

Lynn took a turn with the binoculars and watched for signs of a small ship that might come to their aid. She spotted three stacks—the ship itself had not rounded the curve of the earth. How was it possible that the smokestacks appeared to be moving closer together, crowding each other, overlapping until finally they merged into one fat column? The ship had turned—either it was sailing directly away from them, or it was coming closer. Too many times someone had yelled about a dot on the sea or a low cloud in the shape of a sail, and too many times their hopes had been foiled. But the foolish optimism that is the plague of youth is also its salvation.

Within a few minutes, the hull of the ship appeared above the thin line that separates sea from sky. Yes, this freighter was moving their way. Tom fished into his pack and brought out the small mirror he had tucked into a pocket. While he flashed light toward the boat, the marooned friends debated. Tom said someone should take the dinghy out to meet the freighter. Kim considered it a waste of the fuel that held what little hope they had. Besides, the motor had been running on a single cylinder for the last ten days. Garry Wayne reasoned that the freighter couldn't get close enough to the island, and they'd have to use the boat. Tom felt they were wasting precious time—they had been on the island nearly three weeks and unless someone took action, they would surely die and their bones be picked clean by birds and sand crabs. He offered to take the boat. If the engine failed, he would use the paddle.

Kim said it was useless, even dangerous to take a sputtering dinghy out to a freighter over a hundred feet long. But Tom insisted. He had not known Kim long enough to recognize his was the final word. Although his insistence was not meant to be a confrontation, Tom nevertheless stood his ground against Kim's mettle. Rich wielded the swing vote. Usually he deferred to Kim's judgment, but now he gave Tom the go-ahead to take the dinghy.

Tom coaxed the engine to life and pointed the dinghy's nose toward the monstrous vessel. By hope and grit, he managed to steer the floundering aluminum to the freighter's port side and yelled up to the captain a plea to liberate his miserable company. The captain gave him a half hour to get back to the island, break camp, and ferry his woe begotten comrades back to the freighter.

The ship was a 160-foot barge that ferried goods to Weipa, a mining town in the northwest corner of Cape York. Why the vessel had veered off its course could only have been by divine intervention. The vessel was smaller than the other freighters that usually navigated the channel. It had delivered its cargo ahead of schedule, and the captain offered the crew the option of heading home early or diverting into the shallows of the reef for some fishing. While the men summoned mackerel to their hooks, they grew curious about the flashes of light from an island that was supposedly uninhabited and maneuvered the ship as close as they dared go, about two hundred yards off shore and just close enough for Tom to reach them in the dinghy. Once the foundlings were aboard the freighter they discovered walk-in coolers stocked with surplus ice cream and cold drinks, to which they helped themselves. A crewman informed them that it was New Year's Eve. They had been on the island nineteen days.

No one talked much about the Houghton Island ordeal. To acknowledge how close they had come to death might have set a curse on them—they were young and would not entertain disaster. Tom and Lynn went on to New Zealand, and the Rosebud farmers went back to the land. The Cape Trib men told Kim that the tugboat driver thought Kim had made other arrangements to be picked up, and they hoped he was still interested in sharing the lease on the island. Kim was furious, but he held his peace and said he would fare better by putting his money into building his own boat rather than investing in the atoll.

By the time Charlie Dean meandered from Japan to Kuranda that spring, the Houghton Island incident was all but forgotten. Rosebud Farm had a grove of pawpaws, a pineapple patch, a field of corn, coconut palms, passion fruit vines coffee plants, and banana, mango, orange, grapefruit and lime trees. Vegetables sprang from the ground, and the air was fragrant with flowers, wood fire smoke, compost, and sweat. Charlie had come to refresh his spirit by connecting with the earth and with old friends, and they welcomed him with open arms.

CHAPTER 9

No Worries

Everyone must learn how to fall before they learn to fly—
must drift in the wind before setting their sails.

—Paul Simon
from Harry's journal

O ut the airplane window, the new Sydney Opera
House looked like clamshells washed up on a beach.
Harry had read about it. The Danish architect,
Jorn Utzon, stumbled onto the design when he was cutting
up his grapefruit one morning, the peel falling into wedges.
Because of a political dispute with the Australian government, Utzon left Sydney before construction was completed.
Queen Elizabeth was due to arrive to dedicate the buildings
in a few weeks, but Utzon would not come even then. A
pity, Harry thought—the structure was magnificent. Behind
the white shells, skyscrapers reached into the southern
hemisphere. Sydney was urban—from a distance, not much
different from Boston—and not at all the frontier Harry
had imagined.

From the airport, he caught the train into the city
and checked into a room at a cheap hotel. His body was
still on East Coast time. He'd lost twenty-four hours when

he crossed the International Date Line somewhere over the Pacific. He was a day older here, a day closer to the opening of hockey season. An autumn without hockey—already it seemed strange. He would have to invent a persona without skates, a new and improved Harrison Gardner Reynolds.

Sprawled on the narrow hotel bed, he finished the biography of Humphrey Bogart that he had started reading on the plane. The son of a doctor, Bogart had high ethical convictions. He had grown up in New York City and had gone to Andover Academy in Massachusetts, not far from where Harry grew up. Bogart was direct, simple and honest, and he made decisions on his own terms, even if he ruffled some feathers. Harry would follow Bogie's example, except that he would try not to ruffle anyone just yet.

He dozed off and awoke hours later, hungry and confused. Australian sun shined through the curtain. How long had he slept? His stomach dragged him out to find something to eat. At a newsstand, he checked a paper— Tuesday, August 30—and looked for a good book. He still had a long trip ahead to get to North Queensland. Kenneth Cook's novel *Wake in Fright* caught his eye, a story that takes place in the outback, which seemed an appropriate introduction to this new territory. Then he found a respectable-looking pub, ordered a "sanger"—a sandwich—and a draught of bitter and opened the book. What he found in the novel was more disturbing than entertaining. A schoolteacher, Jack Grant, finds himself in a desolate outback town. When he drifts into a raucous gambling den, Grant gets caught up with locals whose primary interests are boozing, fighting and hunting. The ruffians convince Grant to join them on a midnight kangaroo hunt that turns into a drunken bloodlust. In the morning Grant confronts the horror of his savage instincts and wanders the desert in a state of hallucinatory madness, a victim of his own self-entrapment. When Harry put the book down, he wondered if he had walked into a nightmare of his own making. If this trip turned out to be a disaster, he had no one to blame but himself. But there was no turning back now. And besides, what did he have to turn back to?

Two girls sat down at the table next to him—his age, maybe younger, blonde and brunette, both pretty.

"No reason to sit by yourself, eh?" the blonde said, patting the bench next to her.

Harry tucked the book under his arm and joined them. They introduced themselves as Jackie and Yvonne and said they worked for the gas company in Sydney.

"What's your name, then?" Jackie asked.

"Jack," he told them. Cook's novel had made him wary.

Yvonne said, "Yew a Yank?"

Harry stared down at his book. He wasn't sure how to answer—how did they feel about Americans?

"He must think we bite," Jackie said.

"No worries," Yvonne said. "Have a pint on us."

He liked their nasal Aussie accents, the way they ended every sentence with a rising inflection, their lack of pretense, their uncomplicated acceptance of him.

"Not an anarchist, are yew?" Jackie asked.

The anarchist movement was building around universities in Sydney and Melbourne, they told him. Young anarchists painted graffiti on billboards and stole milk off the stoops of fine houses to distribute to the poor. At a "freestore" in town, people could shop for used goods with no charge. Radicalism had found its way to Australia.

"No," Harry said. "Not an anarchist."

Yvonne wanted to know if he was a "raver"—if he partied—and she and Jackie talked about "slags" and "tossers" and "wads," which he gathered were types of people he was not to emulate. Australia was becoming as liberalized as

America, it seemed. Eighteen-year-olds had just been given the right to vote. Three years earlier, in the largest demonstration in Australia's history, two hundred thousand people protested the war in Vietnam. The U.S. had just legalized abortion, and he wondered if Australia might follow that action. In that case, he might just get lucky.

Everyone Harry had met so far was friendlier to him than Bostonians would have been to a stranger, and he was starting to feel that he'd made the right choice to come halfway across the globe. But when Jackie asked where he was headed and he told her Kuranda, Yvonne declared it "the arse end of the world." He considered staying longer in Sydney, but he was eager to see his old friends. Before they left, the girls gave him their addresses and phone numbers and invited him to call the next time he was in Sydney.

That night, Harry bought a train ticket to take him as far as New Williamsbah. From there, he'd have to pay another fare for the rest of the way to Cairns. The wood-paneled compartment seemed charmingly old-fashioned, as if he had gone back in time to the antique elegance of the old American West. The train creaked around curves, and the whining of the rails was an incantation for sleep.

In the morning he looked out, expecting the desolate nothingness for which Australia was famous. But cows and horses grazed in meadows and kangaroos scampered from the train's whistle into green brush. Except where the train tunneled through mountains, the sky was broad over pleated hills. He passed ferny rainforest ravines where palms mingled with pines. Farmhouses scattered themselves over grasslands and cattle gathered at watering holes. Small country villages were no more than a few bungalows snuggled up to a tavern.

It was hot at eleven a.m. when Harry arrived in New Williamsbah, ninety Fahrenheit at least. He got off the train and stretched his legs. The mountains had given way to parched fields cleared for sparse cattle nosing hope-fully for grass. What an odd feeling to be in the middle of nowhere—but there was also an undeniable sense of release that comes with the first hours of freedom, a buoyant sensation that made him giddy-headed. At the same time, he was almost smothered by apprehension. His bag held $950 in traveler's checks, and his wallet bulged with bills he'd cashed from his checking account, minus what he'd spent on hotel, food and train ticket. What if some drunks wanted to give him an experience like the one Jack Grant had in the novel? He'd never be able to reason with them—talk was not his forte. At least he was big enough to fight them off if they wouldn't take no for an answer. But he'd avoid a fight if he could. He didn't want to depend on his muscle and bulk. It was time to develop other aspects of this flesh and intellect and psyche he called self.

His cash would have to last him a while, so instead of shelling out for the fare to Cairns, he decided to ride on his thumb the rest of the way. He was in no hurry, but he would be cautious, only get into a car with a single driver, avoid crowds and be polite. Jack Grant had fallen in with the wrong people. That wouldn't happen to him if he kept his wits about him. Besides, he was eager to soak up some local color.

For five days he hitched and slept just off the road, too tired to worry about scorpions, millipedes, and deadly-fanged slitherers that might warm themselves against him. Each morning he awoke gratefully unbitten, the fragrance of orange orchards sacheting the dry air.

Everything in Australia was backwards. Cars drove on the left side of the road, and the weather got hotter the farther north he traveled. Most of his hitches were short hops, and once, while he was waiting for a ride, two detec-tives stopped and searched him for marijuana. He didn't smoke much and would never have tried to smuggle dope into the country. Nevertheless, he'd have to watch himself.

The drivers who picked him up seemed glad to talk and distracted him from the flat scenery. One man bought him a pint and a sanger at a bar. The women's liberation movement had not yet reached Australia and, not allowed inside, women sat in pick-up trucks sipping beer from bottles while the men went in to drink. Another hitch carried him a full day from Nambour to Gladstone, about six hundred miles. During the ride, the driver poured out his heart.

"I run off from the missus, eh," he said. She was mulish, running his life, he explained, and he'd put up with enough. He hadn't been gone three days when she filed a missing persons report, and he was on his way back before the law came after him. "But be some bloody mammoth changes, eh," he warned.

On a second day-long ride, the driver was on his way to Townsville to look for a job. He'd left his wife in Brisbane, but she'd join him if he managed to find work. Both men were amiable and generous with conversation, and they told Harry he was "a good bloke."

Harry had read a little of Australia's colonial history, spanning back two centuries when the first convicts—tough men with nothing to lose—scratched a pitiful living from the land. Aussies were bighearted if they liked you—biased, bigoted and brutal if they didn't. He was a long way from the Owl Club, that was for sure. More than a shower and a good night's rest, he was looking forward to the comfort of a familiar face.

When Harry arrived in Cairns on Saturday after-noon, a flock of green parrots squealed overhead. Low-voiced birds with calls like steel drums sounded the same five melodic notes. Tenors joined in and then shrill flutes. Mountains by the water's edge looked like shadowy giants squatting to drink. The sky mirrored the turquoise of the Coral Sea, and the air smelled of nature's industry—fish and bird and root and sea bottom where the tide had receded. Harry felt as if a film had been lifted from his eyes. A white shirt was blinding, the glint of metal nearly unbearable. He could not drink his fill of purple and scarlet of the tropical flowers blooming beside the boardwalk. What was this place that held such truth and purity in its colors?

But he would have plenty of time to explore Cairns. Now he wanted to find Rosebud Farm. The road to Kuranda wound up through the tablelands around hairpin curves with barely enough room for two cars to pass. Scarred and rocky and covered with scraggly trees, mountains rose straight from the road on one side and dropped off in sheer cliffs on the other. His ride—a trucker on his way to Mareeba—dropped him at Speewah Road, and he walked from there over a single-lane bridge and onto Douglas Track. Kim had written directions—he would find Rosebud at the end of the road.

Giant fichus stood sentry at the driveway, which ran under a canopy of palm fronds. Philodendron vines draped from trees like green snakes. An iron fry pan leaned against the trunk of a banana plant. A towel and tee shirt hung on a line strung between post and tree. From one of the fields, a brown arm waved under a broad-brimmed hat, and white teeth flashed in the bright afternoon. There was no mistaking that picket-fence smile—but Charlie Dean was the last person Harry expected to meet in Kuranda.

CHAPTER 10

The Rosebud Project

And who's going to be the one
To say it was no good what we done?
I dare a man to say I'm too young,
For I'm going to try for the sun.

—Donovan
from the Rosebud Farm journal

In the five years since Harry had seen Charlie, the St. George's School Senior Prefect had undergone a radical transformation. His hair now fell nearly to his shoulders, he had grown a bushy chestnut-colored beard, and there was an unruly look about him, as if he were celebrating his wild freedom. Shirtless, he wore a necklace of leather woven with a shard of dried bone, and his skin had turned brown under the Australian sun.

There were years to catch up on, but first Charlie showed Harry to the bunkhouse. The accommodations looked like an army barracks, unpainted walls with a metal roof and no insulation. Outside, leafy vines ripe with passion fruit spilled over the bank. The bunkhouse lacked electricity, and the bathroom was an outhouse thrown together behind the building. It was certainly a big change from Winthrop House, Harry's senior dorm at Harvard, with its crown molding, twelve-pane windows, and fireplaces in every common room. He had some acclimating to do.

Curious about the newcomer, the other residents filtered in. Jap was stringy and quiet, and Garry Wayne had a compact muscularity with a flash to his eye that warned not to cross him. Colin was handsome in a wild sort of way that turned gentle with his daughter Clare. Assorted short-term visitors didn't bother giving their names. Heather assigned Harry to a corner bunk, and he unloaded his gear.

Kim came in wielding a wrench—he'd been struggling with a water pipe. Leaner than when Harry had seen him three years earlier, Kim was sinewy, his hands veined from physical work. Even with a bandana tied around his head, he had the air of an aristocrat. His beard and hair had been trimmed and there was nothing angry in his eyes, no sense of rebelliousness. It was as if the feral territory had tamed him. Rich was on an expedition to Southeast Asia, Kim said, checking out the flora of Indonesia and Malaysia, but was due back any time.

Rosebud policy was that visitors could stay as guests for three days, but on the fourth day they were put to task. In commune fashion, the farm was designed to be a self-supporting enterprise, labor traded for room and board. In the three months he had been at Rosebud, Charlie had tried his hand at nearly every job on the farm. After some food and a tour of the property—the Top House, the fields, the compost windrows, a makeshift greenhouse—Harry was made useful. The Willys Jeep needed maintenance, and the tractor had to be rigged with a grinder to grind wheat into flour. The wild pigs they had caught needed tending and the chickens wanted almost constant feeding. Planting, weeding and harvesting were ongoing. The only food to purchase were dairy products—butter, milk and cheese. Eventually they would have a milk cow so even those could be produced on the farm.

Having grown up in New York, Charlie had come to Rosebud without any farming experience, and he was still in a period of apprenticeship, bending to the tasks with the same good humor as high school days. His spiritual duties had bowed to earthly ones—his robe and the cross he bore to the altar of the St. George's chapel had been replaced with cut-off chinos and a well worn hoe. He and Harry were the newcomers, the least adept with the shovel or hammer, and although they had not been close in boarding school, they stuck to each other like best friends.

Kim enlisted the two to help install a water pipe from the top of the stream to the bunkhouse for showers and drinking water. He had always seemed poised on the edge of something, ready to jump for the thrill of the plunge, but now Kim funneled his energy into projects, into whittling, welding, and sculpting a livable home in the bush. Charlie and Harry had only known Kim in the atmosphere of wealth and luxury, where etiquette and comportment dictated speech and behavior. Here, wit and invention came before courtesy. Kim had rigged an old lawn mower engine to run a washing machine, and the water pipe ran into a copper holding tank that fed the washer and a shower. In order to take a shower, a fire had to be lit under the copper to heat the water. The water then siphoned into a canvas bag that spilled into a bucket hung from a cross beam between two posts and spilled weakly through a pierced rose in the bucket's bottom, but once the copper was hot and the bag filled, there was hardly enough water to rinse off the soap. Mostly, Charlie and Harry bathed in a pool that had been dammed in the stream.

Fortunately, Jeb and Garry Wayne had seen to it that the Top House was equipped with running water. Heather took charge of the kitchen. A confident woman with brown hair that fell straight to her waist, she could do anything. Almost always a twenty-liter pot of spaghetti sauce simmered on the woodstove and bread was rising or baking for field hand lunches. Her oatmeal was hot when the farmers gathered for breakfast. She tended the flock of chickens—chooks, she called them—that produced fifteen eggs a day, plenty for the farmers, and omelets were regular fare. She hulled soybeans and somehow made them appetizing, shucked corn and plucked chooks for frying. She roasted large pork pieces in dough on the woodstove to keep moisture in the meat. When fruits were ripe, she pickled and canned. On market days, she rose early to bake sixteen loaves of bread to sell in Cairns along with farm produce. In addition to feeding an army of men, she could get the generator running and find the loose wire in the Jeep motor. Six years older than most of the other farmers, Heather answered to no one—not even Kim.

Gayle was a nineteen-year-old who had grown up in Sydney. She had dropped acid for the first time at sixteen and ran away from home at seventeen. At Rosebud she was called a "blow-in," one of the homeless free spirits who appeared on the bunkhouse doorstep. She lived partly at Rosebud, partly at a commune in Kuranda, or wherever else she could find a pallet or a willing bed mate. When she was at the farm, Gayle took her turn in the kitchen, although she preferred to sit at the big table and write and draw in the farm journal or embroider elaborate designs on patches, which were coveted for decorating jeans. During the day, Gayle was young Clare's most loyal playmate. Clare's mother had taken off without a word when Clare was a baby, leaving Colin to raise her alone. Gayle had a tender sympathy for the girl and took her to the creek where they wove flower garlands for their hair, and she told Clare stories from her own girlhood. A dreamer, Gayle was childlike herself and documented Rosebud's moods in poetic entries in the journal. On one page, she wrote:

Parents: thank you for conceiving me
for teaching me the names of

the sun, the moon
and the stars
of earth, of fire, of air
and water
of life and love
for I call them all
now and ask their blessings on you.

Although the men tromped with their muddy boots into the bunkhouse, the women made them leave their footwear outside the Top House door, and Siegfried the dog was not welcome. Heather and Gayle kept the Top House parlour and kitchen swept and neat, and the food was warm and good. When Harry had trouble getting the fire lit under the copper for a shower, he called on Heather to light it. With three capable sisters and a highly organized mother, he was used to assertive females. Charlie, with three brothers, had had little experience with women. Gayle's ethereal nature intrigued him, as well as her onyx hair, her generous breasts uninhibited by a bra, and her long skirts that hid mysteries. She was social and flirtatious, Charlie's match at verbal jousting, hers spiced with an Australian accent. He enjoyed having her around.

Rich returned from Southeast Asia wearing a gnarly fedora, denim overalls, and a growth of wild whiskers. He seemed more robust than he had back in Cambridge—Australia agreed with him. His month away from the farm had filled him with descriptions of Timor, Flores and Java, and he spouted about the beauty, the lushness, the kindness of the people. It was incredibly cheap to travel and subsist, he said. Charlie peppered him with questions—had he gone to the Khmer Republic? Had he seen Laos? Was there still fighting? But all Rich wanted to talk about were the tree species, plants and vegetables not available in Queensland. He had tried to sneak seeds of Asian fruit trees through customs, but officials confiscated all but the few he had stuffed into a deep pocket.

With Rich back, talk revolved around rain, drought, weeds and the care of vegetables and flowering trees. Would the seeds germinate in Australian soil? Would the plants thrive? Would they produce fruit? Everyone had an opinion about what should go into the compost stew, but Rich did the dirty work. When they went to Cairns, he haunted the wharfs, waiting for deep sea fishing boats to come in with vacationers. After a wealthy tourist had had photographs taken with his trophy marlin, Rich offered to dispose of the fish, and he cut it up to fuel the windrows of compost.

The richest compost ingredient was donated by the chooks. Rich scraped droppings from the chicken yard and recruited Charlie, Harry and Garry Wayne to help solicit manure from neighboring farmers. The farm truck had an extra long bed with wooden sides chest-high, capacious enough to hold a ton of fowl excrement. Most farmers were delighted to have their coops cleaned. Rich shoveled the reeking booty into buckets, and Charlie and Harry formed a brigade, passing the buckets along to Garry Wayne, who tossed the malodorous treasure into the truck. To keep it interesting, they switched positions at each coop, working their way from farm to farm toward Mareeba and then south to Atherton. When the truck was half full, the fertilizer had to be pitched higher, and the dust from the dried dung flew up, settled in their hair, and coated their sweating bodies. Between farms, three rode in the cab, the fourth balancing on the rank cache, steaming with heat and buzzing with flies. Harry took the first turn in the back, and when he had endured the reek as long as he could, he knocked on the cab window, and Charlie traded positions without a word of complaint. At Atherton, when they stopped to wet their throats with pints of beer, the locals hooted and hurled insults at the "stinking hippies." "Rosebud Farm," Charlie wrote in the commune's journal, "Farm of peace and chickenshit."

Unsavory as the compost tasks were, Rosebud's fertilizer was the envy of tableland farmers, and Rich could grow just about anything with the black gold. Where a Harvard boy from Delaware had learned so much about crop cultivation was a mystery. He had read books and talked to farmers, and he was quick and eager to learn. He took to gardening as if he'd been born to it. He knew to soak palm tree seeds and bury them in damp sphagnum moss in a closed container kept at even warmth until they germinated and that potassium and calcium would help them thrive. He knew to watch for the first roots to emerge and then to plant the seeds in small pots until they were hardy enough to be put into the ground. He knew that summer was the best time for germination and that he'd have to watch the seedlings closely once winter arrived. Before the wet season, the plants would be ready to go into the ground.

Rich's interest never extended far from the gardens. But when people came to the farm, he took them in, extending a warm hand. He sensed goodness in people as he did the new palm shoots—a gentle nature, an appreciation for what was around them—and he could find common ground for conversation with anyone. It seemed right that Rich took pleasure from digging his hands into the earth. He was humble, shouldering more than his share of the work. There was a stoutness to him, like a nut crammed with meat, a seed packaged with economy and potential.

The farm labor was hard and dirty, and when the farmers came together for meals the peaceful coexistence at the heart of the Rosebud operation showed itself at its most fragile. Talk revolved around "fucking tractors, fucking tools, fucking weeding, fucking work." There was bickering about who had not done a shift in the fields, who had not fed the farm animals, who left a mess in the common room, who was taking too much responsibility, who was not taking enough. Some farmers wanted thanks for fixing machinery and others expected appreciation for tilling and planting.

Small and wiry, Sneakers was unschooled but wise enough in life experience to imagine himself an expert in agricultural management and foolish enough to try to take the Rosebud reins. He was scrappy and bellicose, a David standing up to Kim the Goliath. Jap held an opinion on every issue. Garry Wayne was a tough bloke with a competitive spirit. He would fiercely defend one viewpoint, brutally attack another. His temper flare-ups were routine, and Heather described him as "a dog pissing on a post." Harry cut a wide swath around him. He was playing on the Aussie's turf and he would not incite a conflict. Charlie, on the other hand, intervened when Garry Wayne threatened to get out of hand. He had a calming effect on Garry's sizzling nature, engaging him in philosophical debate, cooling his passion with intellect, much the way he'd handled the boys at Carrboro House back in North Carolina. Instead of talking down to Garry Wayne, Charlie made him believe he had something to contribute. He could build things and fix engines; he was good at field work and a natural hunter; he had guts and grit, and Rosebud needed him. Charlie convinced Garry Wayne that he was part of something bigger than himself—something worth protecting—and that responsibility brought him back to his senses.

During the day, while the farmers tamed the wilderness, its wildness seeped into them, and at night it fought its way to the Top House table. They interrupted, dissented and spat invective, their voices rising in volume as egos ignited. When discord reared its head, Rich retreated to the fields or took up a book on soil nutrients or the generation of hybrids. He had no patience for, nor interest in, power struggles.

Kim would not give up in a dispute. He was willing to invest money as long as the farm ran according to his vision, and he was generous about meeting the needs of those who worked. Jap needed parts to fix the machines and Garry Wayne and Heather argued for cash to buy tools and supplies. In a way, Kim was the sovereign of the group, and the supplicants pleaded their cases over soybean stew.

In the East Coast society from which the American boys hailed, it was considered bad taste to discuss finances with anyone but the banker who handled one's trust fund. But the Aussies knew nothing about the mores of Yankee nobility. In Harry's case, there wasn't much money to talk about. When he left Cambridge, he had $22.88 in his checking account and a bit more in savings. He wrote to his father asking him to use the residue in his checking account to cover the nasal spray and photo developing he had charged at a local drugstore and then to close out the account. He had spent five precious dollars on antibiotics after a cut developed into a tropical ulcer, a sore that ate into his leg like acid. His ear, too, had to be syringed when it festered with infection from bacteria he picked up swimming in the Barron River, after which he was deaf for a week. He worried about his money holding out and about his ability to make an impression at Rosebud Farm and in the larger world.

Charlie, however, threw himself into whatever drama was at play. His experiences with the Carrboro house and his leadership in the McGovern campaign had taught him diplomacy, and he had learned to mediate debate. He called on speakers one at a time, interpreted and rationalized. No one person was more important than another, he reminded them. They each had to shoulder their share of the load. To make Rosebud work, everyone had to respect the well-being of the whole community before personal desires. There was a higher purpose at stake than profit or personal security. With an almost mystical ability, Charlie managed to negotiate compromise among the conflicting personalities. He was a natural politician and brought perspective to the table.

In spite of the dissonance, Kim was committed to operating the farm as a model of communal living. Most of the time, debates moved to the pub in Kuranda, where they worked themselves out over a few brews. After one dispute, Kim wrote a poem in the farm journal:

ONE AFTERNOON IN THE PUB

In the pub one hears of a seed.
At home later he shares the story...
another acquires the seed
another buys some pots
another germinates the seed
another gathers sand
another makes compost
another pots the young tree
another rakes mulch
another slashes mulch
another clears a spot
another digs a hole
another plants the tree
another waters and
another waters and
another weeds and weeds
others shovel chickenshit
another bought the truck
others bought the land
another fixed up the truck
another baked the bread
others built the house
another bought the stove
others unload the truck
another spreads chickenshit
another weeds and
another waters and
another weeds and weeds
another mows and mows
another slashes and
another rakes mulch and

another spreads mulch
another weeds
another mows
another spreads compost
another spreads goat shit
another spreads cow shit
another spreads pig shit
another cooks and cooks and
another cooks and
another washes and
another sweeps and
another plays music and
another plays music and
another and another and
another spies the flowers
another spies the fruit
another picks the fruit
now
wait a fucking minute
doesn't   everybody
have
the right
to say
that
the fruit is......
everyone's
big + small
large + tall
fat + short
little + skinny??

The world outside the farm was tangled in greater issues than weeds and compost. The Watergate scandal was heating up in the U.S., and Nixon's presidency looked to be in serious trouble. Pinochet's armed forces had ousted Salvador Allende, the democratically elected head of Chile. With an international fuel crisis, oil appeared to be running out. But Rosebud was secluded from the troubles of world politics. The farm members had the luxury and the freedom to speak their minds and to think and act as they wanted without worrying about balancing a budget or making a profit. Most were trying to find the boundary between idealism and self-interest, a line that in their early twenties was hazy and elusive.

When peace settled again around the Top House table, someone composed an ode to Rosebud lifestyle in the farm journal:

SONG FOR RICH

Well, the veggies have gone off to market
The lady's at home bakin' bread
I'm comin' home from a pig-run
Smellin' like somethin' dead.
Life on a farm is full of adventure—who needs those bright city lights?
Chicken-shit to fill up our days—bullshit to fill up the night.
And after dinner an ale or two
Just to quench my thirst.
I'd like to sleep in my favorite chair
But the pigs have got there first.
Life on a farm is full of adventure—who needs those loud city-sounds?
I'd rather spend a day with my friends and sleep at night with the hounds.

For most of the residents, Rosebud was home and the people who lived there were family. The alternative, after all, was to leave and search out another living situation. But the stalwart stayed and after breakfast together, all hands, even those from the most elite circumstances, fell to their assigned tasks with little grumbling.

CHAPTER 11

Big Mama

If each mortal could only become a focus of dynamic affection, this benign virus of love would soon pervade the sentimental emotion-stream of humanity to such an extent that all civilization would be encompassed by love, and that would be the realization of the brotherhood of man.

—The Urantia Book
from the Rosebud Farm journal

At the head of Speewah Road stood a ghostly leviathan. Imprisoned in a frame of crisscrossed timbers as big as a gymnasium and nearly the height of the surrounding gum trees, the massive boat looked as if it had been dredged from the sea, its hull decomposed to metallic lace with form but no substance. Sunlight shined through it and burned geometric patterns on the packed ground. It appeared that some weighty construction was underway.

The year before Charlie arrived in Kuranda, Kim regularly flew back to Darwin to play baseball with his old teammates. In shooting the breeze, he told them about his father's game fishing cruiser, kept at their Boca Grande house in Florida, and about the big fish he had hooked in the south Atlantic. He would build his own boat some day, he told them. One of his mates knew a couple of Darwin men who were working on a cement boat, and he took Kim to meet them.

A cement hull was new technology in those days but good for vessels navigating the Coral Sea. It held up against the sharp reefs, which rose unpredictably to shallow depths. Even a bullet fired from a rifle would ricochet off a well-built cement hull. Barges had been built of cement during World War II, but few pleasure boats were made of the material, even fewer of the dimension these Darwin men had in progress. The boys, Jeff and Dennis, were using a pattern for an ocean sailing cruiser designed by boat builder Richard Hartley. The French had patented the method in 1855 as Ferciment, in which the hulls were constructed of steel wires covered with a heavy plaster. The British, New Zealanders and Canadians promoted cement for amateur boat building, calling it Ferro-cement, but it was just catching on in Australia. A similar Hartley ship built by a group of young Australians had recently won the Sydney-Hobart race that year, a 630-nautical mile course from Sydney Harbor to Tasmania—one of the most grueling ocean races in the world.

The materials were cheap and no special tools were needed to build a Ferro-cement hull. Jeff and Dennis told Kim the boat would cost around $25,000 to set afloat. Kim was daunted neither by the expense nor by the scope of the project, and he liked the men. The Hartley plans called for a 57-foot craft with a sixteen-foot beam, the fourth biggest Ferro-cement boat ever built in Australia. A vessel like the Hartley would handle the roughest waves the Coral Sea could offer. In a ship of that proportion, they could explore the whole northeast coast of Australia and get a close-up look at the coral reefs, where they might catch some good-sized fish. Maybe they'd even take an excursion around the world.

With a draft of eight and a half feet, the ship's displacement would be 45 tons. Its two cabins, divided by the cockpit, would sleep a dozen guests, not counting the crew. In the course of construction, the boat would consume nine tons of sand, eighteen tons of cement, two miles of steel wire, eighty thousand wire ties, forty sheets of eight feet by four feet square wire mesh, thirty-five hundred square yards of half-inch chicken wire, six and a half tons of scrap metal, and tens of thousands of screws and bolts. In light of her demands and in homage to the old VW Kombi Ute, Kim named the vessel "Big Mama" even before building began.

Jeff and Dennis agreed to come to Kuranda to get the project started, and Kim paid them $75 a week each for labor and expertise, a fair salary for the time. They cleared a construction site near the main road, which allowed easy access for tools and equipment, and a crane would have plenty of space to lift the boat for transport to Cairns when the time came. The first stage was a shed structure 32-feet high and 80-feet long made from square timbers and six-by-four studs of penda hardwood. The boat's frame would hang from the rafters until it was secure enough to stand on its own, so the shed had to be sturdy—eleven rafters at eight-feet intervals. A series of tarps over the rafters would shield builders from the Australian sun.

Locals and gawkers gathered to watch the shed-raising. Transients staying at the farm lent a hand, including a South African named Barry, a quiet young man who had just recently arrived. Dennis supervised as the tall ends were erected and braced into place. The long sides were assembled on the ground. When they were ready, Dennis climbed atop one of the end units and shouted instructions as the farm tractor raised up the first side by way of ropes and pulleys. When the side was vertical, men propped it with stays and Dennis climbed on to bolt it into place. His weight must have dislodged one of the stays, and the huge panel folded back toward the earth like a giant slice of bread cut length-wise along the loaf. Dennis rode the timber down and rolled off just before it landed, which saved his life. Barry, wanting to be helpful in some way, was standing too close.

The young live in a sort of fantasy, especially in the face of disaster—if they don't acknowledge tragedy, it isn't part of their reality. In the transitional time between boy and man, they feel protected, as if looking through safety glass windows from invulnerable bodies. By the time Barry realized that he was not in fact invincible, it was too late to dodge the heavy post that had him in its sights. The timber opened his skull, exposing his brain. When the ambulance arrived, Kim rode along with him to the hospital.

The visitors to Rosebud were seekers, casting their webs wide, looking to connect somewhere. Barry had been a stranger to Rosebud, not there long enough for the farm to claim him as one of its brothers. Sneakers said the accident was fate. Kim, always practical, declared it tragic, but Barry had lived. The misfortune shouldn't interfere with the farm's functions, he said, and construction began again.

Once the shed structure was finally secure, metal rods were hung, forming seventeen trusses spaced exactly 38 inches apart. Jeff and Dennis directed the adjust-ment of screws and nuts until the frame was dead in line and then had volunteers reinforce the components with angle-iron fixed to the frames with U-bolts. Pipe was shaped and welded to the bottom of each frame piece along the horizontal from the rear of the keel to the transom, spaced far enough apart to allow the passage of the propeller shaft. Finally, the transom was overlaid with yards upon yards of square mesh to form a clas-sic curve. Within a few weeks, the ship's skeleton took form—a transparent giant.

Completion of the frame called for a celebration. Kim, Rich, Jeff and a few others chose to head to a Kuranda pub. Dennis preferred to go swimming at "The Boulders" south of Cairns. Kim had told him about Devil's Pool, where colossal boulders split into deep crevasses and dropped off in sheer cliff walls to a deep crystal well. The trick was to jump from the 40-foot cliff and paddle to the side before the watery tongue licked the swimmer through a chute. The funnel, sculpted by eroded rock, sucked the river into a hole shaped like an underwater bottle standing on end. Plummeting from such a height, it takes a minute to surface, enough time for the current to sweep a young man into peril. If a swimmer were unfortunate enough to be caught in the bottle, the force of the water would hold him there indefinitely.

Kim and Rich had been to Devil's Pool over a dozen times. One hot summer day Kim had jumped first and swum to safety. Then he watched Rich pitch himself from the cliff, saw his brown body disappear into the well, surface near the chute and slip like a slug into the drain. Kim scrabbled onto the rocks at the swirling river's edge and waited, eyes fixed to the water's surface. Finally—too long, it seemed—a hand appeared, fingers just breaking the water's crust. Whether it was reflex or grit, Kim's hand was around Rich's, yanking him from a wet grave onto solid ground.

Rich enhanced the story by telling Dennis the aboriginal tale of a princess who died in the river and whose spirit tried to trap young men in Devil's Pool to accompany her in the afterlife. The best swimmers plunged in and fought their way to safety; the weaker fell prey to the princess's desires. No one knew how many bachelors she had claimed.

Kim's warnings made Devil's Pool all the more appealing to the Darwin boy. He was hearty and vigorous and looked forward to hurling himself into the water and bragging that he had escaped the princess's clutches. Ready for a bit of stimulation after the monotony of the boat construction, a group of Rosebud visitors went with Dennis to the river.

Everyone was in fine humor that day—they had made good progress on Big Mama. She would be a fine boat, and they congratulated themselves. Their bodies smelled of metal, and they looked forward to a baptism of air and water.

At the top of the cliff, Dennis paused and looked down at Devil's Pool. He was a good swimmer and most likely gave no thought to the danger of the chute at the pool's edge. When he jumped, the current almost immediately sucked him through the funnel and down into the bottle and pinned him under the rock ledge. In those last moments, Dennis must have seen the light above him, but, as tough as he was, as dexterous and as skilled, he could not fight his way toward it. One second he had known the thrill of the leap, the joy of flying through the air, the electrifying shock of entering the water, and the next his life poured out just as a whirlpool gushes down a drain.

On the rocks, the others watched the water foam, but no one dared dive in—no one dared offer himself as a sacrifice. How many minutes passed, no one could say. There was a time warp before divers and Cairns police came, so someone must have gone to call them.

Bland-faced officers supervised as the divers went under and dislodged the body, dragged it from the water and laid it limply on a stretcher. They carried the stretcher to a hearse-like vehicle made from an old reconditioned Cadillac, slid it into the back and slammed the door closed. How swiftly disaster struck, and how quickly the aftermath was cleaned up and swept away.

Except for Kim, no one at Rosebud knew Dennis very well—his last name, his age, where he was from or his parents' names. There probably should have been some sort of recognition for the work he had done, the time he had spent at the farm, his sojourn on earth. At the very least, there should have been someone to mourn for him. But Rosebud shared an understanding that to be part of its society was to take risks and be ready to pay the cost of those risks. For Barry and Dennis, the cost had been dear.

After Dennis's death, Jeff stayed and finished the hull as agreed. The decks and cabins he left to Rosebud workers. The following year, when Charlie and Harry moved into the bunkhouse, Big Mama was a cause of discord. The boat was a waste of time, some said—they were operating a farm, not a marina. Big Mama was a financial abyss—the money could be better spent on farm equipment. What did Rosebud need with a boat—the farm was in the tablelands. And how could they focus on planting and harvesting if half the workers were off at sea?

It was true that some of the Rosebud company looked to the earth and the others looked to the sea. Sneakers argued for Big Mama. He knew next to nothing about boat building and had never even been on a boat, but he was keen to call the shots. He criticized the supporting structure, the framing, the competence of the work crew. Even though he had quit school and left home at fourteen years old, his intelligence had thrived. His jaw was fuzzy with whiskers and disheveled curls wound about his face. But his thin lips and bones, like glass shards under his skin, suggested the fury that too often worked its way to the surface. His anger kept anyone from getting close to him. He joined the Rosebud residents for meals, but at night Sneakers preferred the more private accommodations of a teepee to the chatter of the bunkhouse. Nevertheless, he insisted he would be an able foreman for the building of Big Mama. He swore they had enough hands to see the project through, even without

Dennis and Jeff, and vowed that if Kim fronted the money, he would keep the workers on task.

Rich groused that he had as much as he could handle with the fields and the fruit trees and vegetables. Then there were the chickens, the ducks, the pigs—and the buildings needed attention. Big Mama would compromise what little manpower he had.

Kim was not about to abandon Big Mama now, nor was he going to turn her over to Sneakers. Most of the labor was donated, often in exchange for food and lodging. He hired a local carpenter to do woodwork on the boat, including building the massive rudder. But it looked like the cost was going to exceed the figure Jeff and Dennis had estimated. Although initially Kim had enlisted a financial partner for the boat project, an Australian named Dale, he carried the bulk of the expenses himself, and Big Mama was no cheap date. The American dollar was worth 68 cents in Australia at that time, but Kim's resources seemed unlimited. Harry recalls once going with him to the bank and retrieving a check for ten thousand dollars from Kim's father. The boat, Kim insisted, would be built with his money and according to his plans.

Rosebud was supposed to be a brotherhood, a model for cooperation and peaceful industry in a time of turbulence in the world. Many of the young men sojourned on the farm rather than fighting in the jungles of Vietnam two thousand miles northeast of where they germinated seeds and hoed furrows. Their mission was to show that peace was more productive than war and love more powerful than hatred. What were they doing bickering over tasks?

After endless debate, it was decided that each of the farm's three financial leaders would focus on his own passions. Jeb would do his woodwork, Rich would tend his fields, and Kim would focus on Big Mama. Kim summed it up: "Rich stayed in the dirt, Jeb stayed in the wood, and I stayed in the cement."

When Kim and Rich came to Australia as twenty-year-olds, they may have been rebelling against their parents, against their social status, and against American politics. But now, at twenty-three, that rebellion had altered into a vision that committed them to the land and to the boat. Big Mama stood as a symbol for how big that vision was.

As visitors who had not invested in the Rosebud project, Charlie and Harry did as they were asked. At the construction site, chickenwire was overlaid with more chickenwire, forming a rigid three-inch mesh that had to be tied together at every crossing point. The two newcomers shared shifts, one on the outside, the other inside the hull. Harry would weave a wire through the cross point, Charlie would twist the ends, trim and hammer down the points, and after a while they'd switch roles. The task seemed less tedious with a comrade to work with, and Charlie entertained them by prattling about world news he'd gotten in letters from home. Egypt and Syria had recently attacked Israel. OPEC had agreed to an oil embargo against Western countries that supported Israel, and Americans lined up at gas pumps. Those with license plates ending with an odd or even number would get specific days of the week to purchase gas. Cars waited bumper-to-bumper around the block. Most stations limited purchases to ten gallons and closed their doors on Sundays. Gas prices shot up from thirty cents to over a dollar a gallon. Charlie was in favor of developing renewable energy sources, using wind, water and solar power and weaning developed countries off oil—especially the U.S. "It's time to stop raping the earth," he said.

While the American government was giving tax breaks for the use of alternative power sources, Rosebud had set itself up as a model for conservation and environmental awareness. Kim's idea for Big Mama was to devise an engine run by methane, made by chemically treating animal dung. For a boat the size and weight of Big Mama, he would have to convert tons of chicken droppings, and the farm already had its hands full of manure with Rich's compost. The alternative was a diesel engine, a suitable compromise.

But the engine would wait until the ship was farther along. When the wiring and twisting were done, Big Mama's hull was ready for its concrete coating. The chickenwire had been covered with half-inch bird netting, five overlapping layers on the outside of the hull and five on the inside. The cement filled in the mesh in a thick, solid wall. Once the concrete set, supports were fastened under the keel so the ground could start taking the weight rather than have the whole structure hanging from the tent's rafters.

Kim had made his own adjustments to the design. He would have cement tanks to hold drinking water, a roomy galley and plenty of storage for fishing gear. He wanted a wheel, a nice one—Australian mahogany with upright handles like the old schooners had. Kim had the focus of Noah, and Charlie wouldn't have been surprised if pairs of pythons, goannas and wallabies climbed aboard.

But by the time Harry was ready to leave Rosebud Farm four months later—even by the time Charlie would depart the following July—Big Mama would still be unfinished. The deck and cabins still needed to be plastered, one painstaking section at a time. The rudder had to be fitted, and the engine had yet to be installed. The interior work still needed to be done. Bills continued to pile up. It would be another four years and thousands more dollars before Big Mama would be ready to sail.

Neither Harry nor Charlie would be around when Kim applied for the license from the department of transport to take the ship to the harbor. They would pass up the dramatics of the crane, a beast with a two-hundred-ton lifting capacity that hoisted Big Mama and transported her, with police escort, around the steep turns down through the tablelands to the Cairns harbor. They would miss the launching and the euphoric realization that, after endless months of dreary labor, Kim's dream was finally afloat.

CHAPTER 12

Respite

mushroom madness –
(islands of golden threads
starships
moons of longing
waxing, waning)
—mountains rising
in its grasp.

—Gayle Hannah
from the Rosebud Farm journal

The barrage of rain on the top house tin roof sounded like the rumble of a didgeridoo, the long wind instrument played by the aborigines. The origin of the didgeridoo comes from the story of ancient times when a giant kidnapped two young maidens to make them his wives. When the maidens escaped and fled back to their village, the giant came after them. Villagers dug a deep pit in his path, and when the giant tumbled in, they came to the edge and hurled spears at his chest. As the giant died, he curled into himself and blew on his penis, making a low, mournful drone like thunder. To the aborigines it was the sound of the giant's power, and they searched for a way to reproduce it. They found a tree limb hollowed out by white ants—Australian termites—and when they blew into one end, they heard again the drone of the dying giant. The sound of the didgeridoo is said to be the echo of masculine strength.

For Charlie, the giant—the most commanding and authoritative presence in his life—was his father. Even ten thousand miles away, he could hear the thunder of his father's voice. He had not seen Big Howard for nearly a year, and he missed what he had resented most about his father—his strict morals, his insistence about backing up ideas with logic and action, and the way his father demanded from him his best. But Charlie was not ready to go back to New York—not just yet. He had to accomplish something first. What that accomplishment was to be, he did not yet know.

Rains came and swelled the creek. The ground was saturated and there would be no field work this day. Nothing was to be done except head to the Bottom Pub to wait out the downpour. In the old days, Kuranda had been an outpost for timber workers and opal and sapphire miners, but now it was overrun with young transients, some of whom stayed at the commune in town. They hitchhiked or came on the train that ran from Cairns. The Kuranda station was a combination of tropical bungalow and flower garden, surrounded by palm trees and planters bursting with greenery hanging from the porch eaves. The red train screeched its whistle as it ambled along the mountain on iron trestle bridges, disappearing into a tunnel and emerging on the other side to heartstopping views of the Barron Gorge.

A trip to Kuranda always promised an encounter with aborigines. The Kuranda natives were from the Murri tribe, part of the indigenous people who made up less than three percent of Australia's population. It had been only six years since the aborigines were given Australian citizenship, and they were far worse off than the mainstream, their lives marked by unemployment, illness, poverty and violence. It was not surprising that as the American men sipped their ale they watched Murris stagger drunkenly down the main street. Because North Queensland was always warm, no buildings had windows, just openings to let in as much breeze as possible, and Murris stopped at the windows to extend a palm for a handout. Always a handout was given.

Long before colonialism, maybe even when natives first inhabited Australia in 50,000 BC, the aborigines called themselves "Bama"—people of the rainforest. At riverbanks they dug for fishing worms using handmade tools painted in stripes of black for the color of their skin, yellow for the sun, and red for the blood their people shed when white men came to their land. They did not know alcohol until the whites settled, but now, for many, drink was their god. When they had had a few, some aborigines got belligerent. Fights broke out among them, and often they'd provoke an Aussie into throwing a punch. Up until 1950, it was not a crime to kill an aborigine, but now the fights were sport, and usually someone bought them drinks once it was over.

Even though the rain had not let up, a skirmish started outside the pub. This one was brief, and no one from Rosebud jumped in to stop the fight—not even Charlie, the best negotiator of the group. This was not his culture, and he would not play peacemaker here. Besides, it was safer to let them play out until one or the other gave up in bruised exhaustion.

When the excitement was over, Kim ordered a second round and then a third, while Charlie held forth on current politics. What little he was able to garner came from *Time* magazines Rich picked up in Cairns when he delivered produce to markets. Vice-President Spiro Agnew had resigned after pleading no contest to a charge of income tax evasion. Nixon replaced him with Gerald Ford, Republican Minority leader in the House of Representatives. At the same time, Nixon's own income tax returns had come under investigation. The firing of Attorney-General Elliot Richardson, Deputy Attorney-General William Ruckelshaus, and Special Prosecutor Archibald Cox was labeled the Saturday Night Massacre. Nixon was ordered to surrender the Watergate tapes.

As far as Charlie was concerned, Nixon was a criminal. But from Rosebud, the American political scene seemed far away and irrelevant. The farmers were less inclined to deliberate with Charlie than to escape into a movie at the community house. For seventy-five cents, they could sit on folding chairs and watch an old John Wayne western projected onto a sheet hung against a wall, snow-capped mountains reminding the Americans of home.

When the weather cleared, the Aussies sought another form of escapism. After a downpour, Jap and Sneakers drove the pick-up around farm roads looking for blue meanies—psilocybin mushrooms that sprouted from piles of wet cow manure. Centuries earlier, the same hallucinogenic fungi had been used by Aztecs during religious ceremonies to communicate with the spirits. But for the farmers, the musky treasures were less a spiritual experience than a free trip. Within an hour after eating a mushroom, heart rate increased, followed by hallucinations lasting up to four hours.

Heather had the job of drying the mushrooms on the roof of the Top House when the sun was out, but she declined to ingest any herself. She didn't like vomiting, which brought on the hallucinations, and avoided drugs while her belly began to ripen with Garry Wayne's baby. Harry once ate a mushroom and felt as if he had left his body, floating outside himself and observing the party as if watching one of the old movies. Comfortable in his huge shell, he didn't like the disembodied numbness, and he never took the blue meanies again. Charlie chose not to try the mushrooms. Beyond a couple of beers and a bit of pot, he was not interested in altering his consciousness. But he did enjoy watching the women trip and dance naked, their skin aglow in the lamplight.

The American boys knew enough to pace themselves, but the Australians showed no such restraint. One young woman downed so many mushrooms that the toxins sent her into a fit of hysteria. She ripped at her clothes and ran around the Top House screaming, out the door and into the yard. Gayle chased her, gathered her in her arms and stroked her head—but it was a long time before she calmed down.

The raving upset Charlie. He had deep-seated ideas about the way women were to behave. His model was Karen. She was intelligent and gentle natured; she had high ethical standards and liked a good joke. If he had stayed in Chapel Hill, something might have developed between them. Charlie had not had much intimate experience with women and was still getting used to breasts bared around Rosebud campfires, women uninhibited with their language and their sexuality.

But Charlie was not a prude. Marijuana was a crop staple of the farm, and he smoked his share during long hours at the wood stove stirring coffee beans as they roasted. Although Kim gave a nod to growing the weed for use by farm members, he absolutely forbade it to be sold for profit. He wanted to keep Rosebud's mission honorable. Already customs agents held suspicions that Rosebud was a drug smuggling ring, and the constable kept his eye on the place. No one knew the constable's real name, but Kim called him "Pinky" for his red hair and pink cheeks, and he wasn't about to give Pinky reason to search and seize the property.

By 1973, thousands of communes had established themselves all over the world. Mystics, Jesus freaks, Marxists, and back-to-nature pilgrims were drawn together in mutual interest groups to stake their claim in the counter-culture. Australia was no exception. Kuranda was especially well known for attracting hippies, and one commune in town housed nearly a hundred transients, many of whom found their way to Rosebud for brief stays. There might be eighteen or twenty people at the farm at one time, including mussed-haired youngsters. Rosebud was a living experiment in social and economic idealism, and while there were good times, the work requirement discouraged long stays. But when Rosebud threw a party, everyone came.

"Tomorrow we're having the annual full moon bash," Harry wrote to his parents, "and we're going to eat Barney, the biggest pig of the bunch. He should feed about seventy-five people and we expect more than that—all friends from Kuranda and some from Cairns."

The day before the party, Garry Wayne aimed his rifle at the pig's head and fired. Kim slit Barney's throat and Garry Wayne dunked him into a caldron of boiling water to loosen the hair, which Harry and Charlie then scraped from his carcass. Kim carved him open and cut out his innards. Garry amputated the hooves and wired the pig back together, then impaled him on a metal bar stuck between the teeth, down the throat, tongue drooping aside, through the carcass and out the anus. By midnight Kim had Barney fastened over a fire pit, and he and Charlie took turns rotating him. Fat sizzled into the fire and the pig turned golden, skin crusting and splitting into crackling.

At five a.m., when Kim and Charlie went to the bunkhouse to catch some sleep, the sun was just about to break over the hill. At ten, Gayle roused them. They'd better get out there if they wanted some meat, she said. By the time they rubbed the sleep from their eyes, all that was left of Barney was cleanly picked bones.

"Mayhem," Kim called Rosebud parties, with long-haired revelers coming and going all weekend. Music flavored the festivities. Popular songs that season were "Reeling in the Years," "Keep on Truckin'," and "Angie." Sneakers was crazy about "Dueling Banjos" from the movie *Deliverance*, and he could do a perfect imitation on his banjo. Before he found his way to Rosebud, he had earned his living playing the instrument and although his edges were rough, he knew how to plunk those five metal strings. Nothing gave him more pleasure—where Sneakers went, his banjo went.

Sneakers's banjo picking summoned Jeb to take up the mandolin. His shoulder-tickling curls held in place with a strip of cloth, Jeb leaned against a tree and strummed. Someone would follow his tune on a harp-like instrument, and Kim would blow harmony on his flute. Percussion might be hands on a bucket bottom, the cluck of chickens or the quack of ducks. Perched on Heather's shoulder, a pet parrot added soprano squawks and Spooky the cat chirped a note or two. The tunes were mostly improv, echoed back from the pines and scrub brush of the rainforest.

The fashion was cut-off shorts or pant cuffs stained with Australian dirt, work boots or bare feet, faded tee shirts or bare chests and bandanas knotted around the head. Charlie acted as bartender, keeping up his lively nattering, and the beer area was dubbed "Chuck's Bar." Music, food, beer, pot, camaraderie—a Rosebud festival.

One party guest, Preacher Barry, a Timothy Leary-type character with an appetite for LSD, was known for dropping a tab of acid and going down to Cairns to "Woolies"—Woolworth's—with a large shopping bag. He filled the bag with wrapped hard candies from the bulk canisters and dispensed it to children shopping with their parents. The youngsters followed him around the store as if he were the

Pied Piper until the manager called the police, who took Preacher Barry off for a night in jail.

Members of the Kuranda town commune recounted the story of when they had begged a marlin from Rich after one of his trips to the Cairns wharf. They had planned to cut it up for their compost as Rich had done, but no one got around to it and the huge fish rotted in the yard. Finally, someone shoved the marlin down the outhouse hole, but the stench was horrific and the flies made the outhouse unusable. One of the hippies got the idea to burn the smell away. He doused the hole with gasoline and dropped in a match. Luckily, he jumped to safety as the outhouse exploded, rocketing wood, fish and shit everywhere.

Kim bought ten waterbed mattresses for $25 each, put them under banana trees in the mowed meadow, and filled them from the stream. The water heated up during the day, and at night they made a comfy platform for watching the stars or for a philosophical discussion. "Meditation units," Rich called them. But their primary function was pleasure.

"Free love" had found its way to Queensland, and Rosebud did its share to live up to the tenet. Women used their sexuality to undermine male authority, and they met with little resistance. Of the men at the farm, Kim had the most success with women. He knew how to talk to them. American girlfriends came across the ocean to be with him. There was a powerful magnetism about him. Although the other men were far from monks, they usually were not so lucky. Except for Heather and Gayle, women came and went, and those who dallied fell into age-old roles. "The men had ingrained expectations for how the world worked," Gayle said. "They brought those expectations with them into the alternative lifestyle—women cooked, washed, and slept with the men." Upholding those expectations, Gayle flirted shamelessly with everyone. She sat on Harry's lap, embarrassing him, and her eyes flickered to Charlie or to Rich. She was voluptuous, in the way a teenage girl can be. Her round body invited the world in and nurtured it with her spirit. She wasn't Harry's type—not at all like Marj in sophistication. Anyway, if he was tempted by her flirtation, he was too shy to do anything about it. Besides, he sensed that Charlie had his eye on her.

Charlie could not deny the attraction. While Gayle cooked dinner one night, he came up behind her and whispered, "When are you going to put me out of my misery?" She told him to be patient; he told her she was driving him crazy. But his patience paid off.

One hot night after a party, Rich, Charlie and Gayle meandered down the meadow from the Top House. The sweet smells of the gardenias and frangipanis Rich had planted mingled with wild lantana from the rainforest, and frogs and crickets sang a courting song. They were all in an amorous mood, and Gayle let them touch her. She kissed first one and then the other, teasing and enticing. When they came to one of the waterbeds, Gayle took off her clothes, lay down and lifted her arms, entreating them both.

Charlie looked at Rich. "Go ahead," he said.

Although not bashful, Rich lacked the confidence to charm women to his bunk. But here was an opportunity lying at his feet.

"You sure?" Rich asked. Charlie shrugged. Rich hesitated. Finally, he said, "Nah," and stumbled toward the bunkhouse for sleep.

For a month Charlie had been waiting, hoping. Now he accepted Gayle's invitation, taking his time and staying until night lifted its shade and let in morning.

For Charlie, talk was as good as sex. He had not confided in anyone since he'd been at Rosebud. No one had asked about his time in Japan, whether he had stopped in

Taiwan or the Philippines on his way to Australia. No one wondered about what he had gained from his travels, the spirituality of the places he'd visited, the nature of the people and their lives. He had kept it all to himself, wrapped and set on a shelf. He showed Rosebud only what Rosebud wanted to see—his political views, his one-of-the-boys good humor, and his admiration for the projects his fellows had undertaken. With Gayle, finally, he took those parcels from the shelf and offered them to her. He talked about his discovery of Buddhism and the capacity to find understanding, love, and serenity within oneself. He told her of his father and how Big Howard had imprinted on him an allegiance to a cause he believed just. Although he could never enlist to fight in a war he saw as unjust, Charlie held fervent convictions about helping people and a craving to act on those convictions. He had to find a way to get involved, and he had some idea that he might find meaning and pur-pose in Southeast Asia. Gayle remembers the sincerity of his voice, his golden curls and his little Buddha belly that pooched over his shorts. When she asked about the POW bracelet he always wore, he said only that it was important to him. He did not discuss politics with her, did not talk about Park Avenue or East Hampton, and did not mention Karen. Even though Rosebud was a place where there were no secrets, Charlie played his cards close. Gayle sensed he was being pulled by some loyalty at home, but she didn't know if that loyalty was political or personal. It was as if he'd made a promise to someone, as if he were already committed. Or maybe she was just not the right kind of girl for a guy like Charlie to bring home. And yet, he seemed happy and content, especially in her company. "He was like a seed dropped into a field, and he blossomed into joy," Gayle said. Did she love him? Yes, probably. There was passion between them, tenderness, and an intimacy

Charlie had with no one else at the farm. During this time, Gayle wrote in the Rosebud Farm journal:

Lady of the rainforest you wrap your arms around me and sometimes you are honey sweet and sometimes you are wild lantana and sometimes you're a virgin and sometimes you run blood and groan and sweat beneath the mighty sun.

In the rainforest, in the company of Gayle, Charlie had found something akin to peace.

CHAPTER 13

Barron Gorge

The land is the mother that never dies.

—Maori
from Harry's journal

Rosebud Farm had a Neverland quality about it. Kim
was Peter Pan, leader of the lost boys. Society was
Captain Hook, the antithesis of youthful dreams,
the adult world whose innocent idealism had been amputated and who was left with bitterness and lust for revenge
against threatening cultures. The antagonists took the form
of Kuranda cops, customs agents, and parents beckoning
their boys home to traditional jobs and traditional paths
toward their futures. But the lost boys were loath to leave. The
mysteries of Australia held the Rosebud company transfixed.

Among those mysteries were the wild creatures of the
bush. Pythons as large as twenty-eight feet long roam free-
ly in the rain forests of North Queensland. They fall from
trees or writhe out of the underbrush, looking for chicken
dinner or small dog lunch. It is a widely known practice for
new parents to sleep with the infant in bed between them
for the first year—until the baby is too big to swallow. In
another ten years, when Jeb became a father, he would be

awakened in the night by his screaming son. He would find the boy with his foot stuck through the bars of his crib, the foot deep within a python's throat. Jeb would pluck the snake off the boy but the teeth would stay imbedded in his foot. One by one, Jeb would pick out the python's teeth, glad for his living son's yelps of pain.

There were taipans, too, the most venomous land snake on earth, twenty times more poisonous than a cobra. But taipans are shy, and barking dogs and grunting pigs kept them at bay. Nonpoisonous pythons were usually welcome at Rosebud to prey on rats that invaded the fruit bin and the oat barrel. An eighteen-footer was the largest Kim had seen on the farm, but the ones who climbed to the rafters of the bunkhouse to warm up on cold nights were smaller. Once in a while a python would exceed the boundaries of its welcome. Spooky chose a lower cabinet of the Top House to bear her kittens, and Heather granted her the space for the cat's help with keeping the rodent population under control. After a few days of nursing her young, Spooky yowled a racket that brought Heather to check on her. A python was nosing close to the kittens. Heather yelled for Kim, who snatched the snake away just in time to save the litter. When a snake grew too brazen and slithered under the dinner table for droppings, or when it threatened to make off with a chicken, Kim grabbed it behind the head, threw it into the back of the truck, and drove it to Kuranda. A town farmer would trade a duck for the python, just for the satisfaction of killing the serpent before it summoned its fellows toward his flock.

If Kim were feeling compassionate, he would donate the snake to Stan's Zoo in Kuranda. Stan kept toads, turtles and snakes for tourists to ogle. The gift of a python granted Kim a half hour with Stan's book, H. F. Mac-Millan's *Tropical Planting and Gardening*, a comprehensive encyclopedia of every plant that can grow in the tropics. The book, published in 1933, was illustrated with colorized photographs of the Perdinia gardens of the royal palace in Ceylon, the most beautiful tropical gardens in the world. Ceylon was five degrees closer to the equator than Kuranda, but Kim saw no reason Rosebud's gardens couldn't rival those of Ceylon's royal palace. If he and Rich were going to have an agricultural enterprise, its model should be no less than the best.

While Kim was walking the fields one afternoon, he caught sight of movement in the brush. He knew at once it was a python, a big one, and he lunged for the tail. Charlie was weeding a row of soybeans nearby, and Kim yelled for him to help stretch the snake out. Charlie declined.

"Harry," Kim ordered. "Take ahold." Harry had never held a python, or any snake, for that matter. He'd thought them slimy, lowly creatures, but he would not be a coward. He took the tail from Kim, and Kim worked his way to the front, grasping the python behind the head. The snake was at least twelve feet, as long as both Kim and Harry lying head to foot. Thick as a sewer pipe, it was heavier than Harry imagined—two hundred pounds, maybe more. The skin was not slimy at all but dry and smooth, the scales small and tight.

"Ain't he a beauty?" Kim said. He was, Harry agreed.

Trepidation was not in Kim's lexicon. He courted exhilaration, and his enthusiasm was infectious. It was impossible for either Harry or Charlie to refuse any offer Kim made, even for a hike down the Barron Gorge.

From Kuranda, the Barron River gushes down mountains of rugged rock, cascades over the massive boulders of Barron Falls and dumps into the ocean twenty miles south of Cairns. By road, it is seventeen miles from Kuranda to Cairns, but hiking straight down the river and jumping the falls it is but five miles, easily done in the dry season.

The gorge is spectacular—a cross between the Grand Canyon and Niagra Falls on a smaller scale. Over thousands of years, the elephant-colored stone was gouged out by the river on its way down the mountain range, leaving a wide swath of pockmarked rock like the backbone of some gargantuan dinosaur. Standing at the top, it feels as if the only way down is to take flight.

The territory within the gorge is wild—completely unmarked and without roads or facilities. Australian folklore tells of the Yowie, a seven-foot gorilla-like brute who lives by the river. He supposedly walks upright and emits a foul stench, frightening off competitors for food by grunting and splashing stream water. Hikers have reported sighting several of the hairy beasts along the river —family groups maybe—and human-like footprints in the mud measuring a foot and a half long. But if Yowie existed, he didn't bother the prospectors who popu-lated the gorge during the early 1890s when gold veins were discovered at Tinaroo Creek, the source of the Barron River. The prospectors may have pushed out Yowie, along with whole communities of indigenous people. But on this day's hike, the only precious substance the men saw was reflected in the sun on the stone—streaks of pewter and gold. Any remnant of dwellings—white or aboriginal—had vanished.

During the extreme wet season, the river sprays over the falls into pools 260 meters below. But in the dry season, the water looks more like a silver vein from atop the cliffs. The pools are calmer when the water is low and the slippery and mossy rocks are easier to maneuver. The aborigines believe that the carpet snake Budadji was the creator of all rivers and creeks of the Barron Gorge. When greedy birdmen ambushed Budadji, killed him, chopped him to pieces and threw him into the bush, the snakes came to the gorge to mourn. That may be why the rocks are home to so many snakes, some deadly venomous.

In spite of slithering reptiles and the freshwater crocodiles, Kim recruited Charlie, Harry, Rich, and Garry Wayne for a gorge trek. The five were like mountain goats— agile and athletic. Charlie was different here. In high school he had been the undisputed leader, and the other boys— even Kim—looked to him to make policy, both in student government and in the social sector. But here he was out of his element, a visitor, an outsider, and neither he nor Harry had much clue about the rules of this foreign turf. This was new sport, and there was no doubt that Kim and Rich were calling the plays.

A man in his twenties doesn't worry about injury. There is a fevered urge to put the body to the test. His reflexes are quick. The body's responses to the brain's impulses are immediate. The muscles are toned, the ligaments strong. Caution is considered a weakness, and there is no limit to what he believes he can do.

Charlie stood atop the first cliff of Barron Gorge, a seventy-foot drop to the water. No doubt he thought about Dennis drowning in Devil's Pool and about Rich's close call there. Rich told him that he'd seen his mother's face as he struggled under the water. Charlie had not seen his own mother in eight months. He'd almost forgotten how she looked when he left New York. Would he ever see her again? Or his brother Howard, his best friend? What had brought him to this life, and what plan was laid out for him?

But it was dangerous to think. Better to surrender the will. Kim had jumped first, and then Harry, and they stood on the rocks at the pool's edge and waved for Charlie to follow. The sun was hot, the light sparkling, the air soft. Charlie bent his knees and sprang forward.

The surface of water is so hard that competitive divers often bandage their fingertips. When Charlie broke through, he felt as if he had shattered glass. The water's chill was like glass splinters stinging his feet and legs. The cold surprised him. Within the pool, all was green and silent, and he wondered if he would ever surface. When he found the air, he managed to paddle to the pool's edge. The rocks were slippery, and he struggled to get a foothold. Kim was there, waiting, offering a hand to help him out.

Rich tumbled after Charlie and Garry Wayne came last, but he was struggling in the water. Just as Kim was about to dive in, Garry Wayne got himself to the rocks on the opposite shore, bringing with him a gray-black eel, ten feet long and thick as a muscled arm. He flailed a stick of driftwood at the writhing creature, and it curled from the blows, whipped its bulky body, and finally fell still. But in the battle somehow Garry Wayne had dislocated his shoulder, and the arm, out of socket, angled across his chest looking oddly dead. With no access in or out of the gorge, there was no choice but to keep going down the mountain to get to a doctor.

Harry helped Garry Wayne around the biggest drops. At a wide part of the river, Kim suggested they take a break, and Garry Wayne seemed grateful for the rest. Kim got out his fishing gear and Harry tried his hand, but his line caught on a rock and snapped. Charlie and Rich also came up empty. Kim threw in the line and hooked one almost immediately. Within a half hour, he caught half a dozen good sized barramundi and jungle perch. There seemed to be nothing Kim couldn't do. The American boys had all come from the same backgrounds, and yet Kim had taken to this wilderness. This was not the scalawag Charlie and Harry had known at St. George's. Kim's expensive education was of no use to him here. But he had developed aboriginal instincts that attuned him to nature, and both Harry and Charlie saw him now with new admiration.

When they reached the bottom of the gorge, the farm truck was waiting, and they got Garry Wayne to the hospital to mend his shoulder. Later, when they sat down to a meal of fresh fish and fried eel at the Top House, there was plenty for everyone.

Charlie Dean's St. George's school photo.

Harry Reynolds's St. George's school photo.

Kim Haskell's St. George's school photo.

Kim Haskell, Australia, 1970

Jap at Rosebud Farm

Charlie and his "Chooks"

Heather Smart

Jeb Buck

Rosebud farmers in Bloomfield

Heather and Siggy

Kim and Charlie in Bloomfield

Rich Trapnell

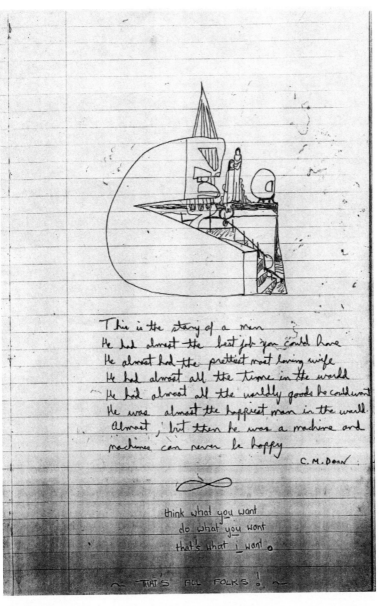

This is the story of a man
He had almost the best job you could have
He almost had the prettiest most loving wife
He had almost all the time in the world
He had almost all the worldly goods he could want
He was almost the happiest man in the world
Almost, but then he was a machine and
machines can never be happy

C. M. Dean

think what you want
do what you want
that's what i want o

~ THAT'S ALL FOLKS! ~

A drawing from the Rosebud
Journal by Gayle Hannah

Big Mama under construction

Jap and a python

Rosebud farmers round up a wild pig

Working on Big Mama

*Jap and Sigfried
at Cape Tribulation*

*Harry Reynolds and
an unknown Rosebud
Farm visitor*

Kim Haskell (r) and an unknown Rosebud Farm visitor

Sneakers, Jeb and unknown Rosebud Farm visitors

Inside the Top House

CHAPTER 14

Bloomfield

[I]t's always seemed to me a whole lot more cowardly for a man to have to do nothing with the meat he eats except picking it up in a supermarket meat section all sliced and boned and wrapped in cellophane, looking about as much like a pig or a cute little lamb as a potato does... I mean, if you're going to eat a living creature, you at least should know he was once living and that somebody had to kill the poor devil and chop him up.

—Ken Kesey, *Sometimes a Great Notion*
from the Rosebud Farm journal

One of the popular books at the Top House was Robert Heinlein's *Strangers in a Strange Land.* Harry felt himself a stranger in this exotic land. A year ago, he was sharpening up the skates for hockey season. He knew the game calendar, he had a girlfriend to watch him play, his class schedule was set, and he felt secure with the routines of his life. He hadn't realized until he came to Kuranda how pampered his life had been. The scent of wood polish and leather from Cambridge days was replaced with the stink of compost, the musk of hot skin, and fumes of pot, spices and roasting meat. Harvard was behind him. He had plunged himself headlong into this lifestyle, and he wasn't about to complain about it, no matter how miserable he felt.

Charlie thrived on communal repartee, but he too was feeling restless, ready to move on to the next scene. He wasn't much of a farmer, and since he had no passion for boats, work on Big Mama did not inspire him. Some days he felt at home at Rosebud, and other days he wondered what he was doing there. He hadn't intended to stay so long. Rosebud was just a fork in the road—he could take a number of paths from here. He still wanted to make his way to Indonesia and Cambodia, maybe even cross the border into Vietnam and see where the fighting had been going on. He owed that much to the soldiers who had made such sacrifices.

As much as Charlie and Harry always had one foot out the door, they both delayed leaving. Rosebud had entered through the soles of their feet, flowed into their bloodstreams and pumped into their hearts. Even though they were mostly spectators of the action, they recognized that there was something exceptional and wonderful happening at the farm. Both Charlie and Harry craved that for themselves—a piece of land they could work and build on and be proud of. The privileged young expatriates were like members of an American nobility, each wanting his own domain to oversee. Unlike Rich, Kim and Jeb, who left college early, Charlie and Harry had gotten a late start. At twenty-two and twenty-three, they weren't exactly sure what it was they wanted. If they continued at Rosebud, they would never be the kings of their own empires. To buy their own acreage in Australia would be imitating what Kim and Rich had done, even if the projects were worthy ones. For the moment, they each tried to find balance in an unsettling ambivalence.

Arguments continued around the Rosebud dinner table. Rich needed more help with the fieldwork. Jeb managed to duck hard labor, which aggravated those who took up the slack. Kim waged constant battle with the Aussies who continued to insist on marketing the marijuana crop for profit. Not even Charlie could make peace.

As a distraction, Kim offered a trip north to Bloomfield. He had bought a large piece of land with Jim Broman, a successful young businessman from Port Douglas. A few weeks on the property would at least offer some perspective on Rosebud's future.

The 3,300 acres were close to the water, remote enough for Kim to be autonomous and close enough to Cooktown for society, should he desire it. And he could harbor Big Mama while he did the finish work on her. A real estate agent had flown him over the property, but Kim had yet to walk on it. The purchase seemed like the right move for him, and he and Broman had each plunked down a $5,000 deposit. The twenty-five thousand from Charlie's father was burning a hole in his pocket, and he thought of stepping in as a partner. But if Charlie were going to commit to a land investment, he'd want Howard involved—he always saw his future connected to his brother's. He decided to wait, have a look at the land, and see if some other opportunity presented itself.

No more threatened by money problems than he was by towering cliffs and gigantic serpents, Kim dived headlong into the hundred-thousand-dollar enterprise. He had a trust fund to back him up, and he could always sell his share of Rosebud, if it came to that. The sales contract sealed, Kim formed an expedition party bound for Bloomfield.

Short-haired and tall-eared, Siegfried was streamlined for blitzing through the rainforest undergrowth. He might have been part dingo, such was the look of the wild about him. Siggy did not acknowledge a master—he belonged to the farm and ate from any hand that offered. He knew enough to stay out of the mid-day sun, curling up under the bunkhouse porch for afternoon naps, if he could convince the snakes to yield their ground. Dogs were valuable property in Australia. They alerted their human friends to danger, they discouraged predators, they kept good company and didn't talk back. Siegfried was first to volunteer for Bloomfield.

A half dozen young fruit trees in pots were packed into the five-ton truck and tarped down beside a small mountain of chicken manure. The dinghy was fastened on top of the manure, along with gasoline, fishing and diving gear, a bag of rice, rolls of poly pipe for a gravity-fed waterline, machetes, tents and camping equipment. Ten of the Rosebud crew climbed aboard—Kim, Rich and Jap up front, and in the back Charlie and Harry, Hap—a new recruit—Colin with young Clare, Garry Wayne and Gayle, the only woman.

The stench from the manure was overwhelming, especially in the heat of the noonday sun. During the two-day drive over bumpy terrain, red road dust sticking to sweaty skin, even Charlie abandoned his usual banter. The tall wooden sides made it impossible to see out unless one stood and looked over the cab. Charlie rode most of the way standing. The truck rattled down from the tablelands through mountains mangy with thirsty trees. In the flats, yellow fringe ruffled from the tops of sugar cane stalks in fields along the road. From Kuranda to Mareeba, tall ant hills stood like tombstones in a cemetery. They passed banana, passion fruit and pawpaw groves and clusters of bougainvillea blooming fuchsia. The white flesh of ghost gum trees glowed in the sunlight.

Long and straight, the road followed a run of the dividing range, crossing dry and cobblestoned creek beds through acres of struggling trees and wheat-colored brush.

Charlie noticed the handpainted sign for Maitland Creek, gouged and cooked to brick in this October spring. His middle name was Maitland, after his mother's maiden name. Perhaps it was a signal for him, a message from home.

Kim stopped for refreshment at Mount Carbine Hotel, which was no more than a rickety lean-to with a cooler full of beer. On its way to being condemned because of white ant damage, it served its purpose to wet whistles and provide some relief from the heat.

After an hour in the shade, Kim headed the truck toward the fifteenth latitude where, closer to the equator, the temperature rose. Pastures were not fenced, and long-horns wandered onto the roads and stood their ground until Kim jerked the wheel to weave around them. Just before Lakeland, they crossed another mountain ridge and looked across Daintree National Park to Mount Boolbun, Mount Pike and Thorton Peak, thousand-meter mountains rising from an arid wasteland.

They camped along the road and the next day took a break at the Lion's Den pub, the oldest drinking establishment in far north Queensland and the only watering hole between Cairns and Cooktown. Crocodile and wild boar skulls hung on the walls, and beer bottles and currency from around the world decorated the bar. The open-air room was crowded with antique tools, graffiti, and a clutter of memorabilia. Young barefoot hippies and leather-skinned Aussies sipped suds, played darts, shuffled cards or watched a soccer game on the telly over the bar. A tan woman in a gypsy skirt offered her handmade necklaces for sale. A scruffy dog rested its head on paws under a table. The Rosebud crew took advantage of this last outpost to wash their dusty throats with a few beers.

From the Lion's Den, the road to Kim's property was no more than a rough path, but preferable to the Bloomfield

Track, which was passable only in the dry season. For thousands of years, the Kuku Yalangi aboriginal people lived beside the Bloomfield Track, which ran along the coastline. Early timber cutters used the track to search for red cedar. One would have to have enormous imagination to call the Bloomfield Track a road. A car could be swept away while fording streams that swelled without warning. Steep hills were strewn with boulders, and the sides of narrow descents without guardrails fell off down precipitous slopes. Not even stout-hearted Kim would wager the truck's axles against the Bloomfield Track's brutality, and so the passengers in the back held on while for three hours the truck scraped bottom over rocks and brush, bucked over rises and rocked around elbow bends.

Except for a few aborigines, Bloomfield was nearly uninhabited. A scant three hundred residents lived scattered over the area with a single road passing through, if one could called it a road. If an oncoming vehicle should want a right of way, the driver would have to veer into the brush and be lucky to gun the wheels out again. But the land was beautiful. At night wallabies poinged in front of the truck's headlights, and red eyes of bodiless creatures stared from the bushes. Kim had a crude map, and when he reached what seemed to be the designated area, he pulled the truck over and cut the engine. On the left, through struggling trees, the Coral Sea glistened under moonlight. The only sounds were the nocturnal whine of insects and the whisper of surf tumbling onto shore.

A path into Kim's property had yet to be cut and it was too late to bushwhack, so the travelers unpacked bare necessities for camping on the beach. They staked tents with driftwood, brown sugar sand squeaking under foot. There was not another soul in sight nor light from a single dwelling. Rainforest rose up behind the narrow beach, shadowy and unfamiliar. Charlie was sure he could hear it draw slow breaths. They spoke softly, lighting a quick fire against the dark. While they cooked and ate, they sipped salt air and measured themselves small against the vastness of the luminescent sea.

By the time the troops rallied the next morning, Kim had already speared the first catch of fish. The Bloomfield pilgrims baptized themselves in ocean water and Gayle lit a breakfast fire. Reef fishing yielded the day's food. Nothing was fresher than fish hooked in the afternoon and served up for supper that evening.

The Coral Sea was sapphire, its surface rippling with liquid crystals. A body floated weightless in its buoyancy. Snorkeling, one might see giant clams, some five feet tall with purple and green lining that felt like velvet to the touch. Curious blue and orange fish nosed close to the face. The young men felt like sleek dolphins, at home by the water. They waked at its edge and were sustained by its bounty. Life was simple—sleep, swim, fish, cook, eat, walk the beach, repeat the cycle, maybe rearrange the pattern for variety.

After a few days on the sand, the group started onto Kim's land, stumbling over rocks hidden by scrub brush. They swung machetes, carving a rude path. Two miles in, they found an open area cleared earlier by timber cutters, although spiky-blade grass had grown up shoulder high. Garry Wayne and Hap chopped what they could, and Colin, Charlie and Jap tromped down the rest to flatten a space for a campsite. They dug a fire pit, erected teepees, and hung their few articles of clothing on skinny tree limbs.

Rich picked sites for the fruit trees. Hap and Garry Wayne outlined an orchard, while Jap began the digging. They set down pipe to siphon water for the trees and for cooking, but luxuries were nonexistent. There was no outhouse, not even the rudest of showers, no cots or chairs, and no table for a civilized meal. Yet, a fresh breeze blew off the sea, and sweet pawpaws and coconuts grew wild. With little effort, the fish were plentiful.

Kim chopped open a coconut and swigged the milk. Red bandana tied around his head and the tallest of the group, he looked regal. "Wyalla," he said. It was the aborigine word for "windy plains." He raised the coconut shell and took another drink. "Welcome to Wyalla."

In the mornings kookaburra laughed and Brahminy kite cried their thin mewing "kweeaa-kyeeer." Nearly as big as bald eagles, the kite spread chestnut wings out from white heads and breasts as they soared and dived for their morning feast. Kim took to tossing them fish skins, and eventually they sat in a tree near the campsite and called to him for breakfast. Plumeria and lantana sweetened the air, already hot at sunrise.

Harry and Kim hiked back to the road, chopping saplings with axes and marking trees to take down with saws so they could get the truck to the campsite. Siegfried dashed in and out of the underbrush, cocking a leg to stake his claim. At the end of one full day of cutting, they headed back toward the small tent village. Siegfried stopped suddenly, perked his big ears, bayed and charged into the woods to a commotion of rustling leaves, cracking twigs and murderous squeals. In a few minutes five wild pigs exploded from the forest, their black hides rippling over feral muscle. Siggy singled out the smallest and brought it down, his jaws clenched on a hind leg. Kim lunged for the other leg and yelled for Harry to use the axe.

"Come on, man," Kim told him, "you've got to do it."

The pig struggled, trying to loose himself from Kim's grip. Harry took hold of the axe handle. He had never killed anything before. He didn't want to kill the pig, but Kim was yelling for him to "do it, do it, do it." He trusted Kim. Since he'd been in Australia, he'd stuck close to him because he knew he'd be safe as along as Kim was near. Now Kim was asking him to kill the pig, and he would kill the pig.

The young swine screamed at the ache of Siegfried's fangs, and Kim tightened his hold. Harry heaved the axe over his head and brought it down on the pig's neck. The blade crunched through white bone and purple tendon. Blood geysered from the wound, splattering his legs. Harry watched as the pig bled out, kicking and running toward death. As much as he felt a quiver of horror at the precision of his work, he could not deny the thrill that rippled through him. How easy it was to kill.

When they dragged the carcass back to camp, Charlie took control. He dug a pit, lined it with wood and burned the wood to coals. In the meantime, Harry and Kim cleaned and gutted the bounty. When the coals were ready, Charlie laid the piglet atop the glowing embers. Covering it with palm fronds, he spread coals atop the meat, kicked in dirt to insulate, and sat guard. All day he could not be persuaded to leave his duty—not even by the temptation of a refreshing swim.

The Australian bush was leaving its mark on the Park Avenue boy. His hair tousled about his head, and sprigs of weeds clung to his full beard. His skin was leather. It may have been for young Clare's sake that he wore any clothes at all, and what covered him was only a pair of thin, tattered shorts. At times he seemed cartoonishly joyous. From a distance, except for his protruding teeth, white as salt, he blended in with the landscape. Charlie was relishing the Bloomfield experience.

At the end of the day, after brush was hacked and piled, holes shoveled for fruit trees and the water line laid, the pig was finally done. Charlie excavated him from the pit and laid him open for a feast. The pork was perfectly roasted through, tender, succulent, flavored with open sky, and the best tasting meat any Rosebud veteran had remembered eating for a long while.

Aside from the pork feast, the daily diet of fish was punctuated with a pheasant which Hap bagged one day with a bow and arrow. Garry Wayne shot another pheasant, his first time using a bow, which made for a delectable stew.

At night the group lay upon their bedrolls and looked up at the foreign constellations of the Southern Hemisphere. There was the Southern Cross, so prominent that it was borne on the Australian flag. Charlie thought about his family back in the States, about Karen Ellis and his friends in North Carolina. He shivered, even in the heat of night, to realize how far he was from home.

CHAPTER 15

Cape Tribulation

Doing the things you fear to do sometimes has the result you hoped would happen, not the result you feared would happen.

—from the Rosebud Farm journal

Kim tied the boat to a massive log at the edge of the Bloomfield River, out of danger of tides and winds that might tip it. Nearly every day that he checked on it, an aborigine woman was perched on a high bank with her granddaughter, fishing. Rosie was the news commentator, the disseminator of local information. She watched the river rise and fall with the tides and reported on the eighteen-foot crocodile that lived in its brackish water. To date, the crock had eaten several dogs and a Shetland pony.

"Croc got another pony," she told Kim one day. In one bite, the crocodile had taken off the back end of the horse.

"Guess he ran out of dogs," Kim said.

"Guess so," Rosie returned.

"What'll he do when he runs out of ponies?" Kim asked.

Rosie looked at her granddaughter, a dark-skinned girl of about eight. Aborigine children knew better than to swim in the river. Then Rosie looked at Kim and nodded toward the dinghy. "Better watch out," she said.

The crocodile was probably more legend than reality, Charlie scoffed. The woman was just trying to scare the Yanks. But when he saw a young croc about five feet long sunning itself along the river's bank, he piped down.

After two weeks in the bush, Charlie had a yearning for some news from the civilized world and Harry yearned for a beer, so Kim proposed a trip to Cooktown, about fifty kilometers to the north. They considered going along the pilot track, a trail bulldozed five years earlier by a group of farmers who thought to increase their property values by linking their lands with Cooktown. The coastal trail, used mostly for transporting livestock, was rutted and badly eroded and had a thirty-three percent incline. Driving the long way around seemed a better alternative.

During the 1800s when gold flowed out of the hills, Cooktown had been a beehive of activity. The first white settlement in Australia, by the turn of the century Cooktown was the second largest township in Queensland with a population of more than thirty thousand. Gold lured prospectors from around the world, a quarter of them Chinese, making an ethnic tapestry of citizens. After the gold was harvested, the population dwindled, and now only a few hundred people lived there. The Kuranda clan made camp on the beach under a pine tree without raising an eyebrow from the locals.

Among the sights they visited was the hill which Capt. James Cook ascended to survey the harbor. From atop the small mountain, they got a good view of Rattlesnake Point, Cedar Bay and the coastline to the north. Some of the original stone houses were still standing. In 1770 Cook had beached his ship Endeavour on the shore after it struck coral on the Great Barrier Reef, and while the ship was under repair, he explored the coast. He named the cape adjacent to the reef Tribulation for all his troubles, and the mountain behind it he named Mount Sorrow—the voyage was not among his most enjoyable. The men hoped Cook's bad luck would not rub off on them.

One clear night in Bloomfield, the moon rose full. The wind was still and the river flat calm. Kim suggested a cruise down to Cape Tribulation. He had not blamed the Cape Trib commune for the Houghton Island episode. In this rugged land, one needed all the allies one could muster, and Kim intended to stay in their good graces. He suggested the group pile into the boat and pay the commune a visit. They packed snorkels, masks, spearguns, and blankets into the dinghy and started out. All they needed to do was follow the coast south for twelve nautical miles.

Two miles into the journey, as if haunted by Captain Cook, the dinghy's engine sputtered, gave out and would not be coaxed to start again. Even if someone had thought to bring a paddle, the distance was too great and the boat too heavy to make headway. Charlie suggested they use one of the blankets to rig a sail, and a speargun served as a mast. Somehow the boat crept back up the river to camp, and Kim was able to repair the engine. Once underway again, he cracked open the bottle of Johnnie Walker he'd bought in Cooktown and passed it around to keep spirits up.

It was ten o'clock and dark as obsidian when they finally arrived at Cape Tribulation, tired, hungry and quite drunk. A campfire sparked on the beach, and they hauled the dinghy up onto the sand and made their way to the fireside where a dozen of the Cape Trib commune longhairs were having an evening smoke. One man stood, his left hand gripping the neck of a guitar. He was handsome with a mane of long locks and an air of cool insouciance. The others held back, waiting as a pack of wolves waits for the alpha male's approval.

The man exuded both an air of danger and a glamour that was nearly irresistible. When he recognized Kim, it was as if two dignitaries of distant villages greeted each other.

"Doug," Kim said, offering his hand. Doug responded with an arm around Kim's shoulder. The others kept their places, watching. Doug was unquestionably the leader of the Cape Trib commune and Kim's equal in commanding respect.

Three women whipped up a meal to feed the famished sailors. Someone from the commune rolled joints and passed them around, and Doug took up the guitar again. Chords and stories and smoke swirled around the beach until the early hours of morning.

The Rosebud group slept on soft white sand under the canopy of a huge eucalyptus. Before dawn, Kim woke Charlie and Harry. Rich was already in the boat, and they wanted company for some sunrise fishing. Rich ran the dinghy through a school of trevally, and each of them hooked good size fish. Kim added a couple more and had them cleaned and frying as the others were rising. Women from the commune supplied a hefty salad, and the day began with feasting.

The view from Cape Tribulation was beautiful. Verdant rainforest yielded to a crescent-shaped stretch of pristine beach. A high, tree-covered jut of land protected the small bay of aqua water. By the forest's edge, squat bushes grew right out of the sand, and in the water low tide uncovered small islands of weedy coral. Charlie dreamed of owning a piece of property like this. On land like Cape Tribulation, he might stay in Australia forever.

The Cape Trib commune had been operating for four years. Neat metal-roofed houses were furnished with tables and chairs that the commune residents had built themselves. The grass was mowed, and a stream by the settlement ran heavy with perch so tame they could be fed by hand. Bush hens pecked around the yard—black birds big as turkeys with red heads, necks and fantails—not very good eating, one woman said, and their gargling was most annoying at night. Cassowaries, cousins to the African ostrich, ruled the woods. Their long necks, a bright melon-color, were crowned with a ridge of bone atop the gleaming blue head. Their huge feathered bodies were powerful. The birds were territorial and aggressive and could knock a man over. One had to be careful when entering the bush to do one's business, as Harry discovered when an indignant cassowary gave him a good chase.

Jap took interest in the commune's pot crop. One building—rigged with the only locked door—housed the dope business. The room had all the apparatus—scales, plastic bags and a label maker. Here the pot was weighed, packaged and marked "Sunshine Marijuana," as if it might be stacked on grocery shelves. The stuff was good, too, if the previous evening's sampling was any indication. Doug hinted that the profits were impressive. Jap told Kim to imagine the improvements they could make at Rosebud Farm with money rolling in from pot sales, but Kim refused to discuss the matter. He would have nothing to do with Rosebud selling marijuana.

The group enjoyed another day of Cape Trib hospitality, which they spent swimming and fishing. Kim and Charlie dove for crayfish hiding in the crevices of the coral boulders. Charlie brought up a monster and Kim speared seven more, providing enough cray for twenty people that evening.

In the afternoon, Jim Broman made an unexpected appearance at the commune. A land speculator, Broman owned some acreage in Cape Tribulation. He was especially astute when it came to real estate investments, and he always had a plan in the works. The latest was some government cattle property up north on Cape York, halfway to New Guinea—139 square miles with thirty miles of coastline on the Pascoe River. All one had to do was to clear and fence a thousand acres for the Australian government in exchange for the right to freehold a hundred thousand acres for one dollar an acre. Charlie still had the money from his father. Maybe he could get Howard to go in with him, and his two other brothers might want a piece of it, too.

As the second oldest son, Charlie no doubt wanted to make his family proud of him. Howard had set the course, and it was a hard one to follow. Already Charlie felt he had disappointed his father by not following Howard to Yale. His ideas were different from his father's, there was no doubt about that. And yet he wanted to show Big Howard that he could make something important happen, something that would make his father see that he was worthy.

Before he settled onto a piece of land, Charlie wanted to see more of this part of the world. But he didn't want to travel alone. He had missed companionship on his trip to Japan and wanted someone along to talk to. Rich had done enough traveling and was planted on the farm, and Kim was tied up in building the ship.

"Come with me," he said to Harry. Harry told Charlie he didn't have the money to travel for a few weeks.

"We can hitch rides, and food costs next to nothing," Charlie insisted. "Come on, man. It'll be an education." But Harry knew he and Charlie were opposites—where Charlie was a social extrovert and ravenously political, Harry was shy and meditative. Charlie sometimes grated on Harry's nerves, and Harry suspected that his silence was unsettling to Charlie. Besides, wandering through Laos and the Khmer Republic—and maybe even to Vietnam—seemed like a radical idea. From what they could gather from news magazines, there was still some residual fighting. Just eight months earlier, Le Duc Tho, the leader of North Vietnam's communist party, had declined the Nobel Peace Prize, saying a true peace did not yet exist in Vietnam. The Australian papers reported that the United States was secretly bombing Cambodia. The war seemed far from over. On the other hand, nothing they had done since they got to Queensland had been safe, and Kim had shown them that fear was a young man's only adversary.

Although they had hopes and dreams, neither Charlie nor Harry resisted whatever the present moment brought. Balancing on the crest of a wave, they gave in to the here and now, which was more vivid and welcoming than the ghostly unknown of the next year or the next decade. Blurred and undefined, the shore of the future grew no clearer as it came. Nevertheless, they would head toward that shore, suspecting that it would either fulfill their expectations or drown them in foolishness.

CHAPTER 16

Black Marlin

To know what is impenetrable to us really exists, manifesting itself as the highest wisdom and the most radiant beauty.

—Albert Einstein
from Harry's journal

At Rosebud Farm, there were no conventions for behavior other than what the young men imposed on themselves, and they reverted back to what they knew, what they had learned from their own fathers. They had a smoke, took a drink, and shared a laugh with their buddies. They kept abreast of politics and sports teams. They provided for their people, building shelters and harvesting crops. And they took on hard tasks that would mold their identities. Even as they criticized the authority and standards of their fathers' generation, they clung to those standards for security and comfort, although they would not acknowledge so. The rules of the rugged North Queensland territory were different from those of East Coast boarding schools and country clubs, but that former existence became their only rubric as they floundered with new guidelines for conduct in this brave new world.

Charlie, Harry, Rich and Kim depended on their alliance with each other—their link to old comforts. All but Kim had been cut loose from their parents. The Trapnells' marriage was faltering, and Rich rarely spoke to his father. Jeb's father was immersed in work and drink. Phil Reynolds was allowing Harry the space and time to play out his Australian odyssey. Charlie was only occasionally in touch with his parents and communicated mostly with Howard. For the most part, the parents gave their sons distance to carve new traditions and revise old ones. Only Hal Haskell came to check on what his oldest boy had created on this island-continent as far from home as he could get. Like a good businessman, Hal wanted some firsthand knowledge of where his investments were going. He wanted to see the exotic coral reef Kim had written him about and to do some deep-sea fishing. Mostly, he wanted to make sure he wasn't losing his son.

When he arrived, Hal Haskell booked a room in a Cairns hotel. Cairns is settled on a jut of land wedged between the Barron River and Trinity Bay, with the Kuranda mountain range rising behind it like a stony specter. In its harbors were sailboats, fishing boats and pleasure boats. Even in 1973, Cairns was a resort city made up of bars, open-air pubs, and gamblers crowding the rails of horse racing tracks. Sunbathers splayed themselves on city beaches, and shoppers eyeballed iridescent opals in the shops along the Esplanade. But the biggest attraction was the Coral Sea, with the largest reef in the world, measuring over 345,000 square kilometers, more than half the area of Texas. Once part of the mainland before they broke off and drifted from shore, over a thousand islands hunched their white sands in the reef.

Cairns was booming, but the development did not please Charlie, who would have preferred to see mangrove, rainforest and swamp dominate as it had a century earlier. In the ensuing decades, white settlements took hold in the region and prospectors mined for gold, copper and tin. By the 1970s, most of the natural resources had been mined out, and the landscape was reverting to its natural beauty. Charlie hoped humanity would let it be.

When Rich joined Kim and his father on the three-day charter for the great marlin hunt, Rosebud Farm declared a holiday. A Canadian named Keith had befriended the farmers and suggested a fishing trip to Port Douglas, a small peninsula an hour north of Cairns where Jim Broman lived. Keith had done some diving for Broman, who owned and operated an international deep-water diving company, and thought he could convince Broman to let them take out his cabin cruiser. Charlie, Harry and Garry Wayne were game for a little fishing.

Broman agreed, and the five motored twenty miles out into the sea without charts or a compass to find a reef where he said the fishing was sublime. Below the window of water, coral hovered like crystal clouds. Above, the wind was calm. On such a day, space, distance and time have no meaning, azure melts into sapphire at the horizon, and blue descends endlessly below and endlessly above.

Charlie spotted a school of big fish and yelled to the others. Quickly they baited hooks and got their lines over the side. Garry Wayne snagged one right away, but it slipped off the hook as he reeled in. Harry outwitted a mackerel, a prize three feet long and weighing at least ten pounds. Almost immediately he landed another, and Keith added a couple more to the quarry.

Eager for a swim, they took turns jumping overboard with speargun and snorkel, careful not to brush up against the hard limestone corals—a gash could be disastrous. Those aboard watched for sharks and box jellyfish, whose tentacles inflicted fatal stings. The blue-ringed octopus, the size of a golf ball with a poisonous beak sharp enough to pierce a wet-suit, could kill a man in minutes. All of the fifteen species of sea snakes on the reef had small fangs with lethal venom, and the barbs on a stingray's tail would cut deep. If any of the men was adept enough—or lucky enough—to spear a fish, there was the real threat of shark attack. So, the trick was to keep out a wary eye, and if you hit your mark, head back to the boat and climb aboard with all haste before the sharks smelled the blood.

Both Charlie and Harry came up empty, but Keith speared six coral trout and caught seven more fish with a line. Broman snagged another fish and three crays. The painted crayfish were menacing looking, with snake-like stripes on spindly legs and white beady eyes pivoting on little pedestals above their heads. Later they went back to Broman's house and indulged in hot showers while Broman's girlfriend cooked up the crays and fried some of the fish. Broman turned on his television to a soccer game. Having lived for months without electricity, much less TV, Charlie was mesmerized by the little characters on the screen. For so long, news of the world outside North Queensland had been abstraction rather than reality. But here was evidence that people were playing sports and going about their business, unaware of Rosebud Farm and its dramas. He watched the players and the commercials for cars and shampoos and cold medicines as if he were a visitor from a distant planet, witnessing earth civilization for the first time. But as much as he found it fascinating, he had no desire to be part of the foolishness.

As the four were about to say their good-byes, Kim and Rich showed up with another pile of fish. They hadn't brought in a marlin, but Kim had reeled in a mess of golden trevally and nanyigai, and so the pan was heated for another course of seafood. Even better than the feast was the news that Hal had invited Harry, Charlie, Keith and Garry Wayne for the next day's charter.

Harry had not seen Hal Haskell since the party at Chadds Ford Farm the summer after freshman year at Harvard. Rich and Web Golinkin were at the party, along with a couple other St. George's friends and one or two of Kim's many girlfriends. Charlie had been in the throes of Chapel Hill politics and did not attend. Hal had wisely made himself scarce while the boys dropped mescaline and roamed the acres and acres of pastureland in a psychedelic haze. But Harry remembers seeing Hal early in the weekend, the sparkle in his eye a sign of his delight in having his son home and his son's friends around. Kim's nature had more urgency and turbulence than his father's, but his father was a man at his best when he was on his property surrounded by family and friends.

When they arrived at the dock the next morning, the 45-foot charter was stocked with sandwiches and beer. A day's charter was two hundred fifty dollars—a hefty sum for that time—but Hal spared no expense for the boys.

Aboard a fishing ship, there is a feeling of anticipation about what lies under the surface of the water. The Great Barrier Reef section from Cairns north to Lizard Island is recognized as the marlin capital of the world. During the summer months, from November until February, black marlin are plentiful. Blue marlin can grow to a thousand pounds, but long line fishermen have landed much larger blacks. Annually the marlin migrate to the reef to spawn.

A giant marlin is a splendid creature, shimmering in the air on a gigantic leap from its ocean home, thrashing the sea's surface, wild and powerful. The boat crew talked about trophies that had been hooked and lost, some after battles that lasted as long as 24 hours. What were the chances of these young prep-school boys catching a trophy fish? They'd had some luck fishing with Broman's boat and held high hopes for this trip.

In the next slip, actor Lee Marvin was getting ready to launch out. He had been an action hero on the television show "M Squad" and in the movie *The Dirty Dozen*, but he was not so impressive in his fishing togs. Compared to the adventures the young men had already experienced in Australia, Marvin's on-screen exploits seemed tame by comparison.

As they motored out of the harbor, Dennis, the boat's captain, threw out a trolling line and pulled in bait mackerel, some a foot and a half long, and stored them in coolers of water to keep them alive. It was spring in Australia, and the air was so perfectly fresh that Charlie wanted to weep for New Yorkers watching dry October leaves tumble from trees, hoarfrost heralding afternoons of early dusk and mornings pale with chilling rime. Was there a more perfect place on earth than in this boat with these friends? He doubted it.

Once they reached the reef, first mate Paul attached a few of the live mackerel along the fishing line and fed them out behind the boat. Then each man took a half-hour turn in the fighting seat, hands alert for the jerk on the rod that meant a hit. Kim tried to coax a fish to the line, to no avail. Charlie sat the seat next, without success. When Garry Wayne's turn was up, he had barely gotten his line into the water when he shouted "Woo-hoo!" and launched himself into battle against a blue marlin. From the way he fought the line, Garry Wayne must have caught a whale— or at least a great white shark. Finally he worked the fish alongside the boat so they could get a look at it. Charlie thought it was a champion, but Paul said the marlin was less than five hundred pounds, still a baby, and they released it back into the sea to grow some more.

Finally Harry was up, and he settled into the chair, eyeing the sea for signs of life. Late morning light reflected bright on the water. He wished he had sunglasses or a cap with a bill. He had drunk two beers while he waited his turn, and the alcohol made him groggy. He closed his eyes and felt the weight of the rod in his hands, the drag of the line through the water. A half an hour wasn't much time, and he willed a big one to notice his mackerel and be enticed to bite.

Harry could have sat all that day and the next. He could have sat a week—the young man and the sea—because he knew as well as he knew when a breakaway was coming and he'd go one-on-one with the goalie, find the gap between the pads and land the puck in the back of the net—he knew that well that a marlin would strike while he was in the seat.

He was twenty minutes into his turn when the jerk came with such power that, without doubt, he had hooked a huge fish. He had fought twenty-pound mackerel that threatened to yank him over the gunwales of Kim's runabout, but he'd never felt strength like what battled him at the other end of the line.

When he hollered, the others gathered by him, yelling directions. Kim checked that the strap around his waist was tight to the chair, but otherwise no one touched him. One rule of marlin fishing is that only the person who hooked the fish can bring it in—no one else is permitted to handle the rod. Harry tried to remember the instructions Dennis had given when they left dock.

"Let him play out until he's tired," Kim said.

Dennis advised, "Conserve your strength."

Harry's eyes were open now, and he saw the marlin sound and dance on the water. His body glistened, his nose knifed the air, and when he hit the water, spray leaped to the sky.

Someone—maybe Charlie—gasped, "Holy mother."

"He's a big fellow"—Hal probably.

"Looks like he might be gut-hooked," Paul said. "Keep tension on the line or he'll throw his stomach." Gut-hooking meant that the marlin had swallowed the mackerel and he'd vomit up his own stomach to get rid of the hook unless Harry kept the line taut.

Dennis said, "Okay, start reeling him in."

The handle was anchored snug in the holster, and Harry leaned the rod back and then reeled like a madman as he bent forward. The muscles of his chest felt as if they would tear through the skin. He braced his legs against the boat's stern and was glad for hockey thighs, for Coach Cleary's wind sprints that had kept him fit. Every ounce of his nearly two hundred pounds was focused on the rod jammed into his palms, his curled fingers stinging from the pressure.

Pull, lean, reel. Pull, lean, reel. The rhythm helped, but the marlin's weight wore on him. He resisted the quivering coming into his shoulders—he would meet the fierceness of the fish; he would be its match. But he wished it would jump again, show itself. He and the marlin were adversaries, opponents, but also brothers on this reef—one in the watery world, the other in the airy realm. But gut-hooked fish have little jump in them; they tire fast. In less than an hour, Harry had him portside. When Paul poled him close, Harry saw the anger in his fish eyes. He knew that look—the indignation of defeat.

"He's a thousand pounds, I'd bet," Paul said. Dennis said he was the biggest marlin ever brought to his boat.

Harry looked at the black bill, the gray-pink of the backfin, the silver of his belly. He was a prize.

"Cut him loose." Charlie spoke. They had all agreed to release any marlin they caught. No one would eat marlin.

Rich had enough to fertilize the compost, and none of them believed in killing a fish for the sake of the prize.

Harry had seen the trophies hanging on the pier and thought his dad would like a picture of him next to his victory.

"You caught him, now let him go," Charlie said.

"He's better off spawning more marlins than hanging on your wall," Kim said.

No one demurred—not even Rich argued. Harry nodded, and Dennis took the cutters and freed the fish.

That evening Hal took the boys to the Hides Hotel in Cairns for a few belts and afterward to a Chinese restaurant for dinner. Harry was glad Charlie had insisted on setting the marlin free. In a way, coming to Australia was like being cut free from the expectations of their parents. They would not be trophies on the walls of their parents' dens—they would explore life's ocean on their own, leap and dance on its dazzling surface. Before they drank, they raised their glasses and delivered a toast to the black marlin.

CHAPTER 17

Aussie Christmas

It is necessary, while in darkness, to know that there is light somewhere,
to know that in oneself, waiting to be found, there is light.

—James Baldwin
from Harry's journal

F or the three months Harry had been in Kuranda,
he had worn the same boots every day. Twice the
soles had come loose and he had sewn them back on
with heavy thread. His clothes were stained and frayed. His
hair had grown over his ears and was curling onto his neck.
Although he kept his nails trimmed, dirt wedged into his
cuticles, and his fingers were calloused from farm work. His
resources—both tangible and financial—were dwindling.

James Michener's novel, *Drifters*, had fallen into
Harry's hands. The story was about six young runaways
adrift in a world of their own creation, colored by dreams,
drugs, and dedication to pleasure. It was easy to confuse
dreams with reality. He didn't want to give up his dreams,
but he needed a dose of reality. Although he was tiring of
the Rosebud scene, he was more convinced than ever
that owning land was the right move. "When I see what is
happening with the land being chewed by fat cats, I know

173

Kim is right, that now is the time to buy and protect this land. There will be schools, shopping centers and work up in Kuranda faster than you can believe. When I see the place at Cape Trib and the land of Kim's both here and in Bloomfield, I know this is it. Getting my own land is my next goal." The problem was that, unlike Charlie, he had no cash at the ready. And so, for Harry, the dream stayed just that—an abstraction that he hoped some day to sculpt into reality.

Charlie was closer to realizing his vision. He could not conceive of living in Manhattan again, and he had severed ties with North Carolina. He might start his own farm or maybe establish a fishing business or invest in some sort of trade with New Guinea. The potential was rich. He'd learned the virtue of hard work, and toiling in Rosebud fields had shown him that with determination he could achieve anything. He thought about the Pascoe River property. The only obstacle was the hundred grand he needed to get the project off the ground. Howard had written that he was willing to go in and offered Charlie his entire $25,000 gift from their father. Charlie now was waiting to hear from Big Howard and his two other brothers. He wanted to share the Queensland experience with his family, to show them the alternative to the snobbery of Park Avenue and the Hamptons. He hoped to set up a Dean family compound, a simpler life where they might build something together.

Kim had taught both Harry and Charlie to experience life and feel its pulse. To survive here, they had to trust themselves and not make judgments based on someone else's advice. And yet, they needed to know how to deal with people, to communicate and be perceptive and compassionate, making sure everyone worked for a common ideal. In a materialistic, capitalist world, Kim always said, there can never be harmony. Greed and hunger for money and possessions overpower integrity and human decency. But how would Charlie ever get Big Howard to understand?

Up until now, Charlie had been a good son, never making trouble or worrying his parents. But he sensed from his mother's letters that his parents thought he was veering from the path they wanted for him—a job on Wall Street and productive use of his education. She wrote news of his classmates getting married, going to graduate school, and landing high-paying positions. He wondered what she might tell her friends about him—my son is living on a commune in Australia while he "finds himself"? More likely she just said, "He's traveling," an acceptable endeavor as long as it didn't go on too long. If he went back to New York, as he suspected his parents would like, he'd be giving up the little independence he had gained in Australia. It would take courage to thwart the hopes his family had for him and to become his own person. He imagined himself twenty years from now, atop his own hill in a house he designed himself. Maybe his children would play at his feet, or maybe they would be grown and on their way home for Christmas. There would be a woman, and he would be comfortable in the familiarity of her presence. If he could have, he would have telescoped across time to get to that older self. Instead, he was nagged by conflict and indecision.

Garry Wayne's birthday was in mid-November. While Heather cooked a feast for the celebration, including a small pig and huge mocha birthday cake, Garry Wayne and Harry put up barbed wire fencing around the fields. In the afternoon they helped Kim, Charlie and Keith take the roof off the boat shed. Then they drove to Kuranda for a few quick brews before dinner. An old miner who had wandered into Rosebud a week earlier had just cashed a check for $23 he had earned from working at a tobacco farm, and he was determined to spend every cent, buying beers all around. With the miner's help, they tied one on, toasting Garry Wayne and priming themselves for a party. Back at the farm, Garry Wayne helped himself to a couple blue meanies, and Charlie set up bar, opening bottles of NQ lager and mixing up a punch of vodka, pawpaw juice and passion fruit. Gayle had adorned herself in a white nylon gown she had bought at a thrift shop and a fake diamond necklace. Charmed by her coquetry, at dinner Charlie put his hand on her leg under the table. "You have an awfully long—arm," she teased.

When Charlie took to his bunk, he thought about how there had been no celebration of Thanksgiving at Rosebud, no turkey and stuffing sitting around the big table as he was sure his family had done in East Hampton. Now the Christmas holiday was just ahead. His mother would find the biggest tree for the family room, and his younger brothers would be recruited to help string colored lights and hang ornaments. He always liked watching the beribboned gifts accumulate under the boughs and toasting the season with glasses of spiked eggnog at neighborhood cocktail parties. No doubt there would be parties at Rosebud, but wild and raucous ones—no navy blazers, no ice cubes tinkling merrily in crystal glasses of scotch.

Keith was moving to Melbourne—he had fallen for a woman who lived there and wanted to see what would develop. Harry said maybe he would go to Melbourne, too, and try to find work. Charlie would have liked to be someplace familiar for Christmas, surrounded by family. For Rich and Kim, Rosebud was home. But Charlie felt no permanence there. No matter how long he stayed, he felt like a visitor. If he could endure through the holidays, he'd make a decision then.

Rain fell for a solid week before Christmas. The sky hung heavy overhead, leeching color from the land so that even the verdant rainforest looked drab. Philodendron vines grew inches daily, coiling around fichus trees, and pink impatiens invaded like weeds. During the day, the temperature climbed into the thirties Celsius—ninety Fahrenheit—and the air was nearly too thick to breathe. The creek overflowed its banks, and Heather, tending to bread baking, was trapped in the Top House. Jeb had rigged a wire to the bunkhouse, a sort of bush telephone, and she called for help. Keith and Garry Wayne threw her a rope, and she tied it to a tree on her side of the creek and used it to balance as she waded across, her belly big with baby and bread bags dangling from strings around her neck.

Cyclone Una crossed North Queensland, killing four people in Townsville and causing massive damage to buildings and fields. The local roads were flooding, and it was tough traveling even to Kuranda village. It was not unusual to get 150 inches of rain from late November to March, but this might have been one of the wettest seasons ever—maybe four hundred inches.

Harry read books and scribbled letters. To his brother Phil he wrote, "Every time you need a shower you just step outside with a bar of soap." His clothes were damp, and the pages of his journal stuck together. He was bored and impatient. The walls of the bunkhouse were squeezing tight. A transient named Jose invited him to play a game of backgammon, and he accepted. He lost the first game, which infuriated him. Why did he have to be so competitive? Charlie's razzing added to his frustration. Big Harvard hockey player can't even win a game of backgammon, Charlie poked. Harry wished he had the verbal poise to spar with Charlie, but he knew he was no match in that arena. He had pledged to change, to convince himself that winning wasn't everything. But it wasn't working. Charlie knew it and took advantage. Jose agreed to a rematch, and Harry triumphed in the second game, but his drive to win robbed him of any satisfaction.

Rain assaulted the metal roof like pellets of lead. If the deluge let up in the afternoon, thinning clouds tempted one to be hopeful. But the respite was always brief. Charlie wrote letters home while Gayle doodled in the Rosebud journal—sketches of mushrooms, dreamy landscapes, naked figures frolicking or meditating. She had an artistic talent and an ear for poetry. "Rosebuddies and Rain and Rainforest and Rainbows," she wrote, "and blue skies and sunshine and moonshine. The moon is nearly full and I too reel on the precipice of total immersion in euphoria." Charlie felt the euphoria too, and his contentment made him put off his decision to leave the farm. Even though he had a spiritual sense that the future would unfold as it was meant to, he still had no concrete plans. Not just yet.

In the meantime, Harry was drawing closer to taking action. He had hoped to stay a year in Australia, but he was ready to renege on that commitment. Rosebud had been good for him, but maybe he was foolish for trying to be part of something so different from his past. His moods were as changeable as the weather—sunny one day, dismal the next.

His musings included the possibility of going to work for his brother-in-law. David Chandler owned the biggest apple farm in Massachusetts, Meadowbrook Orchards, and always needed help. He also thought about buying a farm in Vermont with his old friend Sam Burr. For Harry, this Australian sojourn was a time to hone perspective, getting himself ready to launch into the life of adulthood, but he was torn between following the path he had been taught and doing something completely outside the box. Aware of his shortcomings, in his journal he lectured himself with clichéd imperatives in much the way he psyched himself up for a big game. "Have patience," he wrote. "Look at your future realistically, your talents and your weaknesses weighed with equal candor. Follow your heart but don't get bogged down by sentimentality. Do whatever you do to perfection, but don't expect miracles. Try not to take yourself too seriously."

Garry Wayne talked again about splitting. In no way was he ready for the entrapment of fatherhood and as much as he loved Rosebud, he wanted to leave Heather and the whole baby mess behind. Had it not been for Charlie, he might have disappeared one day. Charlie calmed him down, talked him into staying a while longer. Heather needed him, Charlie convinced him, and Garry Wayne needed to be accountable.

Christmas Eve morning dawned bright with scorching sunshine. Charlie and Harry took advantage of the dry weather to help Rich plant a field of corn and another of soybeans, taking their time between rows by making merry with cigars and glasses of port. In the evening, a party gathered. Walking a log over the swollen creek, the Rosebud contingent took to the Top House to prepare a holiday repast. Harry baked a banana nut cake. Kim killed one of the farm ducks and roasted it, and Gayle made her special gravy. There were fruitcakes sent from family members and beer, wine, whiskey, brandy, rum, and plenty of pot. The mood was celebratory, with music, drink, food and laughter.

After a convivial meal, Harry retreated to the bunkhouse, stuffed presents from his mother into one of his worn brown socks and hung it from the end of his bunk. When he awoke, he opened the gifts. There were games and much needed new socks. His Aunt Ginny and Uncle Tax had sent him the book, *The Best of Life Magazine*. His Aunt Bet sent three cigars, a picture of her riding an elephant on a recent trip to India, and two shirts which, if he decided to go to Melbourne, would do to make him presentable. David had written that he was sending a crate of apples from the orchard, but the box arrived empty, the apples confiscated by customs. One package was marked "To Har from Rosebud Farm"—a new vest. As a present to himself, he mended his old boots again and gave them a good shine.

The bong came out before breakfast, but when it passed his way Harry turned it down. Dope made him feel numb—he couldn't read a book and he felt clumsy. It seemed an effort for him to "sling the shit with everyone." For him, these were times of serious reflection, and he needed to keep his thoughts clear.

Charlie had not given up on the Pascoe River idea, and he was still thinking about setting off for Indonesia, where Rich had told him he could take a train across the entire country for five dollars. Then he could start working his way back to the U.S. after a stop in Nepal and a trek through India.

It was about this time that Charlie recorded in the farm journal:

> *This is the story of a man.*
> *He had almost the best job you could have.*
> *He almost had the prettiest most loving wife.*
> *He had almost all the time in the world.*
> *He had almost all the worldly goods he could want.*
> *He was almost the happiest man in the world.*

If Charlie could not manage to settle down and be happy, he would give in to the stirrings he felt building inside. "The horrors of the Vietnam war are starting to reveal themselves," he wrote in the farm journal. He talked about the skin of Cambodian villagers searing from napalm, the brutal slaughter of children and women, bombings that amounted to genocide. "The truth behind all of society's lies is finally emerging," he wrote. "People will soon know how corrupt the leadership really is." He was priming himself to take action. If only he could get started.

CHAPTER 18

Melbourne

First you must take one step; then another, and another: like learning to walk again—the motion must come first.

—from the Rosebud Farm journal

I t was rumored that Winston Churchill gave his dog a bowl of champagne and a piece of cake every morning for breakfast and that during Walt Disney's autopsy, resin from opium was found in his lungs. Whether or not these urban legends held any truth, they supported the Rosebud theory that life indeed was a romp.

On New Year's Eve, Kim, Charlie, Rich and Harry lugged the dinghy and fishing gear into the back of the truck and drove to the house of a friend in Cairns for a smasher of a party. The all-nighter involved gallons of beer, wine, Jim Beam, Jose Cuerva, and plenty of Afganny hash, mushroom pancakes and pot. Charlie opened a third bottle of tequila and did shots with lemon and a lick of salt. When midnight arrived, he and Harry were sitting in a pancake house, choking down food and coffee to sober up—an inauspicious start to 1974.

When Queensland stopped spinning long enough to let them get to sleep, they rested only a couple hours before

Kim prodded them awake at four a.m. Badly hung over, Charlie looked to be in no better shape than Harry, but they both rallied. Kim had some fun in mind, and neither of them would miss it. At the wharf, they launched the dinghy into a dead calm Coral Sea just as the sun was painting the sky a brilliant orange. Kim was at the helm, fresh and energized. How could he be so spry after a night like they'd been through? Obviously he had not found the bottom of the tequila bottle. This was all the celebration he needed— early morning salt spray, hungry fish under the boat, and some good mates to share it all with.

They motored twenty miles north to Bat Reef, off the coast of Port Douglas. The water was diaphanous that morning, and they dove and fished as the sun rose high. Charlie caught a small tuna and some coral trout, and Harry speared a few fish, but they weren't good eating. Curious sea turtles paddled close to the boat, and porpoises flashed their fins from the water. Reef shark darted close at the scent of fish blood.

That first day of the year was pure enchantment, friends surrounded by the beauty of the sea, doing what pleased them most. In the past almost four months, Harry had grown to love his Rosebud family, and he felt their admiration for his athleticism and physical courage and their acceptance of his taciturn nature. But for him, Kuranda was but one link in the endless chain of his life. It was time to move on.

Early in the morning on Friday, January 4, he rose quietly from his cot. No one was up yet, and he didn't bother to wake them. He had said his good-byes the night before, keeping them brief. Maybe he would be back, and of course he would see his friends again—if not in Australia, then back in the States. He slung his pack over his back, walked to the highway, and stuck out his thumb.

Because of flooded roads, only one or two cars passed, and the heat and humidity made hitchhiking insufferable. Finally he caught a short ride, and then another. By afternoon he had worked his way 87 miles south of Cairns to the town of Tully. Thinking to make better time by rail, he found the railroad station, but he had missed the last train to Brisbane. The next train south wasn't until Sunday, and he couldn't squander money for a hotel room. Fortunately, he had a good book—*Papillon*. He took to a station bench and read about Henri Charriere, sent to a French prison colony for a murder he did not commit. Charriere made up his mind to escape the custody of his captors, even if it killed him. Like the butterfly he tattooed on his chest, Charriere would live free or not at all.

When the sun set, Harry closed his book and curled up on the bench, using his knapsack as a pillow.

The station master shook him awake at five a.m. and told him to take off, thinking him a vagrant. He wandered into town and found a place to eat, writing a few letters over cups of coffee. When the pub opened, he settled himself at the bar with a morning brew and his book. By afternoon he had had several beers and fell into conversation with a friendly bloke at the next bar stool. The man invited him home, and Harry didn't refuse. A meal, a shower and a bed for the night were more than he had hoped for.

On Sunday evening he was back at the train station, waiting for the 1:20 a.m. to Brisbane and wondering if he'd made a huge mistake. Already he was lonely. As he flipped the pages of his journal, a piece of paper tumbled out—a note he found on his bunk the morning he left Rosebud Farm, along with a bag of fruit and some sweet bread someone had left there while he slept. He'd long since eaten the snacks, but he'd forgotten about the note. Now he unfolded the paper and held it up to the evening light. It was penned in Charlie's hand.

Dearest Har:
Just in case we're lost in a dream world when you flee us—
we're sending lots of loving vibes and wishes for a pleasant
and eventful journey and a few munchies to see you through.
Please send us a word or two someday and hopefully we'll
return them. Take care and much loving,
Rosebuddies. Yeh!

Those "loving vibes" gave him nerve to forge on, and he boarded the train for Brisbane. He remembered the words of Plato from a class he'd taken at Harvard and scribed them into his journal: "Music and rhythm find their way into the secret places of the soul." The music of Rosebud was in his soul, but he was ready to find his own rhythms. He wouldn't have minded someone to share a few secrets with—it had been such a long time since he'd felt intimacy.

When the train started up, a young woman plopped down in the empty seat next to him. She introduced herself as Chris and said she'd been on the train when he boarded and watched where he sat, determined to meet him. She was Harry's age—22—and was also heading to Brisbane. In her Aussie inflection she told him she'd been traveling on her own since she was fourteen, when her parents died. She was hoping to make it to New Zealand somehow—on her looks and her wit, Harry guessed. She was brunette and beautiful with a self-assurance that rivaled Marjorie's. Harry felt at ease with her at once. The train seat backs were high enough to give them some privacy, and Chris took rolling papers and some pot out of her bag. She crafted a joint and lit up, taking a long pull, and handed off to Harry. It felt good to get stoned with her, and he loosened up, told her about his plans for finding a job in Melbourne and about how he'd always wanted to see New Zealand. He had heard the skiing was good in the winter and thought maybe he'd take a vacation there before long. He also confided how down he'd been feeling at the end of the Rosebud stay. She told him to groove on his lows—that's when you learn most about yourself. Don't be afraid to feel down, she said. He liked her confidence and her warmth. When she invited him to go with her to Coff's Harbor in New South Wales, a beautiful seacoast, he thought it was a fine idea.

They got off the train in Brisbane and started hitch-hiking. A trucker picked them up, and they rode in the back for a ways. In some small town Harry bought them both a bus ticket, and they scrunched into a seat together, pressed in by a crowd of other travelers. He was comfortable sitting with her, without the need to make conversation, watching out the window as dusk descended and the pastures faded to shadow. Along the edge of a cane field, a farmer drove his tractor, setting the stalks afire with a torch. He was evicting rats, Chris said, to make ready for cutting. Harry felt alight, a glow finally igniting in the gloom.

When they were hungry, they got off the bus and found a place to eat and have a beer. Chris was the only woman in the pub, but no one asked her to leave, and over a second pint, Harry kissed her, the first time he had kissed a woman in four months.

It was early morning when they left the pub and lay down in the grass by the road. She was dewy and sweet, and he drank her in until the sun rose high in the sky. At ten in the morning, heat pressing down on them, a trucker stopped. He had room for one, he said. Chris looked at Harry. She kissed him, promised to wait for him in New South Wales, and then climbed aboard. When the truck rumbled down the road, Harry knew he'd never see her again.

He fought to put Chris and Coff's Harbor out of his mind, to stay positive about the path he was on. When he reached Sydney, he found Jackie's number and called her.

Yvonne had moved out, and Jackie was living with her boy-friend, but Harry was welcome for a meal and a night's sleep. He accepted. Yvonne came over that evening, and Harry struggled to find common ground for talk. With their clean hair and ironed clothes, their urban savvy and shallow conversation, the girls were annoyingly straight compared to the women he'd known in North Queensland. How could he have been attracted to them just months earlier? Had they changed, or had he?

At daybreak he was back on the road, inching closer to Melbourne. "Mexicans," Gayle had called people in Melbourne because the city was so far to the south. Actually, the climate was more pleasant than North Queensland—a dry eighty degrees during the day and a relief from Kuranda's downpours. Melbourne was a clean city with tree-lined streets and acres of green parks. Harry liked the feel of pavement under his boots.

He looked up Keith, who had moved in with his girlfriend Sue. They had a tiny flat, but there was a roomy three-bedroom apartment for rent by the Botanical Gardens. If Harry was interested, they would sign for the space. Harry agreed. To save rent money, two of Sue's friends moved into the third bedroom, which Harry found to be an attractive arrangement.

The Melbourne paper had a few promising job listings. One, selling freezers, required no previous experience. When Harry applied for the job, he was hired on the spot. The company supplied bulk food to restaurants and private consumers, and with costs on the rise, customers wanted freezers to store food they bought more cheaply in large quantities. Ironically, the position was one that suited Harry the least, charming potential patrons into purchasing a large appliance. "What I do is tell people about how they can save a lot by comparing what they spend per week now and what they'd spend buying in bulk. The company sets up appointments for us and we just lay the facts on them. It's also a great way to meet people," he wrote his parents, putting up a good front. The job was not difficult. Customers were interested in the product even before the sales pitch, and Harry traveled with a supervisor, who did most of the talking. One buyer even insisted they drink a few beers with him before they left. When a deal was signed, Harry got a $75 share of the commission.

At quitting time, practically every man in Melbourne headed to the pubs, and Harry made a habit of following custom. One evening he asked a bar mate about the hockey scene in Melbourne, and he happened to know one of the players on the semi-pro team, Grove "Boomer" Bennett. The man told Harry where the rink was, not far from the flat, and that he would find Boomer there, managing the rink in the off season. Harry planned to drop in to watch a practice.

He began to enjoy the feeling of having money in his pocket. Harvard had recruited Sam Burr to solicit donations for the Harvard College Fund, and Harry had pledged fifty dollars a year. In a letter to his father, he included a check made out to Harvard. "You can tell hound dog Sam if you see him that I didn't let him down," he wrote. He enclosed with the letter another check for twenty-five dollars, written to St. George's School.

The income made him feel generous, and the generosity gave him a sense of security. But he quickly learned just how naïve he was when some of the other salesmen appropriated his clients—and his commission. The more he learned about the business world, the less he respected the mad pursuit of money. He pledged to take a different route.

Harry quit the appliance company and scoured the paper for other opportunities. One of them led him to the ice rink. Boomer had been considered the Bobby Orr of

Australia in his younger days. A Canadian, Boomer had tried out with the Bruins but didn't make the team because of his size—at five-feet-five, he was too small. But he was the highest scorer in Australia and captain of the Aussie National Team, which was to play in the World Cup in Grenoble that year for the first time. In addition to running the arena complex, which included a restaurant, pro shop and the rink, Boomer owned two of the eight teams that played in Melbourne. He was also the player-coach of the best team in Australia, the Demons. Boomer took Harry out to dinner and showed him around. Harry must have impressed him because at the end of the evening Boomer hired him at $150 a week to be his assistant in managing the arena and running a clinic for young skaters.

Harry's duties included bookkeeping, general office work, and public relations. Practice for the hockey season was to start the first of March, a few weeks away. When Boomer learned about Harry's college experience, he asked to see him skate. Once Boomer saw Harry on the ice, he waved a contract in front of his nose. But the season lasted until October, which meant that Harry would have to commit to staying through the Australian winter, and he'd miss the beauty of the New England summer. He'd have to weigh the offer seriously.

While he was deliberating, Kim appeared at the door of the apartment. There wasn't much for him to do during North Queensland's rainy season, he said, so he had come to Melbourne to hole up with a couple of "fillies" who had visited the farm a while back. When it hadn't worked out with the women, Kim tracked down Harry and Keith, and they made space for him.

The news from Rosebud was that Heather's baby was due any day, and the plants were going wild in the rain. It was all they could do to keep up with the weeding and thinning. Charlie had not yet made a move, although he talked about it every day. Kim suspected that he was having trouble unsticking himself from Gayle.

He had brought Harry a long and rambling collective letter from the farmers. The first section was penned by Gayle:

Harry's diner, evening shift, Sunday
Dear Boss,

Just the staff here tonight. Sitting at the round table. The juke box is playing Dylan Blonde on Blonde and the punk is rolling green stuff between his fingers and cursing. Just the usual jive. And a bit of a rave. Heather fine: waiting. In fact, we're all fine: waiting. A baby in the diner. What a buzz.

Card games have been played for a few nights running. The "corn dodgers" v. the "yahoo laroog." It's too early to tell, but the corn's up and running and so, too, the soya beans.

And the wet season has hit—pretty sure...there's a certain clik! And suddenly you know. So here we go again. Round again. Up again. Down again.

Gayle mentioned Bloomfield and hopes of going back there, planting, building a house and making rainbows. Bloomfield included Charlie. He wrote:

*Scheduled to hit the road on the 29th of March, but I'm trying to fit in a week at Bloomfield. Kim has a rough itinerary of mine—I'll probably head to Africa in May, and I'd dig to see you on the way. Guess I'll be back in the U.S.A. by next December, but then we already discussed how accurate that might be. Come back here before you split. You'll be surprised how **everything** has grown. If I don't see you traveling, I'll see you in the U.S.A. Until then, take it all lightly and don't lose sight of yourself.*

With love for who you are, Charlie

Kim said Charlie was still thinking about Cape York and wanted to go up and have a look at that piece of land Broman had told him about. However, Charlie's plans were far from solidified. If Harry had agreed to go to Southeast Asia with Charlie, he might have been able to set Charlie in motion, to help him find his path. But Charlie had to find his own way, and Harry was sure he would. It was just a matter of time.

Jap added a short message of greeting to the letter, and Rich penned the finale:

We've planted more corn, done a lot of weeding and lots more to go still. Bought a rotary hoe for the tractor and trailer (secondhand Dodge—beauty). So this year we'll really be moving. We sure all miss you, you son of a bitch.

Rich talked about people arriving and people leaving Rosebud, people planning to come and people promising to return. He ended with hopes to see Harry again before he returned to the States and signed the letter with love.

The Rosebud friends didn't make it any easier for Harry to decide about whether to stay in Melbourne or head back to Massachusetts. Years before, Kim had taught Harry to drive on the Chadds Ford property, had shown Harry how to handle a camera and gotten him into music and gardening. Kim had helped him realize so many little things that he had neglected to think about before. Kim had helped him grow up. But, most of all, Kim had been a good friend. He hated to think of living half a world away from him.

While they bided their time in Melbourne, Kim bought a saxophone—he had left his flute at Rosebud. Harry procured a used clarinet, and Keith added electric guitar for some amateur jamming. When the neighbors complained about the noise, they moved across the street to the park and set up the jam there. Bob Dylan's album *Planet Waves* had just been released and Kim blew "Forever Young" on his sax. Keith's voice rang into the night:

May God bless and keep you always,
May your wishes all come true,
May you always do for others
And let others do for you.
May you build a ladder to the stars
And climb on every rung,
May you stay forever young.

The bluesy ballad and its hopefulness about the future made them all forget for a while that time was moving by. They clung to Ram Dass's "Be here now" philosophy with the belief that the next rung of the ladder was always in reach should they desire to make the climb.

While Harry worked at the rink, Kim made plans to travel to Tasmania. He'd never been there, and the wet season seemed a good time to check it out. He badgered Harry to come along. It was hard to say no to Kim, but Harry's longing for home was overpowering. Kim, Rich and Rosebud Farm would always be there, he hoped. But Harry had to find his own peace of mind.

One afternoon a knock came on the door. It was Sue's sister Anni. She had spent the day on the beach, was badly sunburned, and hoped Sue would let her rest at the flat. Kim looked up from the book he was reading on Napoleonic history and saw the dark-haired beauty. He had never been frightened of anything, but this woman seemed to reach out with her deep eyes and cast a spell over him. For the first time in his life, he felt powerless.

Anni and Kim spent the evening talking. She was in school but not liking it. She had grown up in Melbourne, but she found the prospects of getting a desk job and living in a suburb repugnant. She did not want the life her parents had lived. When she spoke, she looked Kim straight in the eye and exuded a quiet but compelling assurance. This woman was Kim's equal. He would not let go of this one.

Harry's visa was due to run out the last day of February, and he still had the offer to work on David's farm in Massachusetts. Although the idea of playing hockey was tempting, his heart was summoning him back to New England. When Anni agreed to go with Kim to Tasmania, Harry booked a flight to Boston.

Flying to Australia, Harry had followed the sun, going toward the light. This time he flew through the dark. In his journal he scribed, *"So here I am, about to land in Chicago and then on to Boston after six months in Australia.... I've become more sure that farming is what I'm cut out for. Good hard physical labor along with a clean and quiet atmosphere to play my clarinet, build a darkroom, start a garden, learn some carpentry. Whether it happens, who knows, but at least it's a goal and something I didn't have six months ago."*

Thanks to Kim, Rich, Charlie, Garry Wayne, Heather, and all the other Rosebuddies, Harry finally knew what it meant to be part of a community—it meant never being alone, no matter how far away he traveled.

CHAPTER 19

Pascoe River

Our vision of the future flows toward us
Growing clearer as it comes, confirming our expectations,
Or, catching us in error, turns our prophecies to foolishness.

—George Walker
from Harry's journal

I
n April, as the wet season came to a close, Charlie turned 24. He had spent rainy days at Rosebud talking with Garry Wayne about the Pascoe River land on Cape York Peninsula. The territory was wilderness and would need to be tamed, and Garry Wayne had the skills to clear and build. Charlie couldn't live in such hostile terrain without him. Twice a day for the last year Charlie had helped Garry Wayne feed and slop the pigs, an hour every morning and another hour in the afternoon, and he spent that time prying Garry Wayne open, getting him to speak from his heart. He respected Garry Wayne, and Garry Wayne felt that Charlie had become more than a friend—he was like a brother. He'd be glad to partner with Charlie on the Cape York property, but first, he said, they needed to see what they were getting into.

Jim Broman was the broker and knew the area well. He arranged for a bush pilot to fly Charlie up to a landing strip near the property where the owner, a man named Owee, would meet him. Keith had returned to Rosebud, and after Charlie took off, Garry Wayne convinced Keith to come along to Port Douglas and help him talk Broman into letting them borrow his boat. Both men were able and dependable so Broman agreed, and they packed the 21-foot cabin cruiser with supplies and two 44-gallon drums of fuel. The trip would be at least 650 kilometers, about four hundred miles, a voyage complicated by seasonal tradewinds that blew at twenty or thirty knots, roughing up the Coral Sea. Such a trip was no less than a mission of love, and no less than Garry Wayne was willing to risk for his best friend.

With Keith and Garry Wayne taking turns at the wheel, they headed out before dawn, past Cape Tribulation and beyond Bloomfield to Cooktown. They motored due north, crossing between Cape Melville and the infamous Houghton Island. Around Rocky Point, they entered Bathurst Bay and navigated among the Flinders Islands. Running low on fuel, they turned deep into Princess Charlotte Bay and picked up two more drums of petrol at the Annie River marina. Much of the land this far north was national park or aboriginal reservations with small settlements called Moojeeba, Wakooka and Kulla. The rest of the peninsula was simply wilderness and had not changed in millions of years.

The two sea weary travelers dropped anchor at Night Island and gaped at the towering cliffs on the cape's coast. After a good sleep, they started north again, past Lockhart River Mission and Restoration Island at the tip of Cape Weymouth. In Weymouth Bay, with craggy mountains on one side and dense tropical rainforest on the other, they found the mouth of the meandering Pascoe River.

Broman had told them to go ten miles up the river, where they should look for a jetty on the north shore. The water was low, with sandbars just beneath the surface. They managed to avoid most of the hazards, but late in the afternoon with the sun blinding them as it reflected off the river, the keel hit sand and stuck fast. The only option was to jump overboard and drag the boat off. Had they known that the Pascoe was infested with crocodiles, they might have thought better about mucking about in water up to their chests. On this evening, however, the reptiles spared them.

Finally, the boat freed, they searched for a campsite along the shore. Certainly they were not far from the landmark, and it would be easy to find the jetty in the morning. Garry Wayne wasn't sure at first whether his eyes were deceiving him, but as the light waned, he thought he recognized the landing Broman had described. Yes, it had to be the spot. They tied the bowline tight to a tree, found a track and started walking. Broman had said the property was five or six kilometers inland, but by this time it was pitch black and they fumbled forward, stumbling over roots and rocks. After what must have been a couple of hours, Garry Wayne sighted the light of a campfire. Through the bush, he could see Charlie sitting on a log, looking toward the noise coming from the forest. His companion had a hand on his rifle. Keith called out, and Charlie stood up. Then there were bear hugs and laughter and claps on the back. Owee offered them a choice of tea or rum, and both men opted for the rum before they settled down to talk about the trip, the land and the prospects for a settlement.

In the morning, the screeching of cockatoos and fluttering of brilliantly colored parrots awoke them. Owee showed them a bit of the land, leading them in a compass several kilometers wide of the campsite, through lush bush alive with birds and towering ant hills and in the distance, misty mountains wreathed in blue. He told them about the huge crocks that live in the river and how lucky they were not to encounter one. He pointed out a slide in the sand four feet across the belly, the paw marks so wide that Garry Wayne couldn't reach them with arms outstretched. Owee said the creature must have been twenty feet long.

The property was too vast to explore on foot, but Owee had four horses, so the men packed their gear and mounted up. He had only three saddles, and Garry Wayne volunteered to ride bareback. Even on horseback, it took three days to get a sense of the expanse, some of the most remote and wild acreage Australia had to offer. At a bend in the river, cliffs loomed thirty feet high and guarded a pool formed by wet season flow. It was hot, and they took a swim and rested by the water.

Owee had a 120-pound hand line that he attached to a piece of wood and fashioned a lure with some wire. He threw out the line and quickly danced the lure back across the water. In a short time, he hooked a monster of a fish that put up such a fight that even with four of them on the line, they couldn't land him. Charlie, Keith and Garry Wayne held on while Owee backed his horse to a ledge and tied the line to the pommel of his saddle. He gave the horse a swipe to set him pulling, and finally the fish twisted and writhed on the bank. It was a giant barramundi that Garry Wayne reckoned to be six feet long and at least 150 pounds. Before they cut him loose, Owee took his rifle out of the scabbard and shot the fish through the head. That night the men feasted on fresh seafood with plenty for breakfast the next morning. The rest they left for scavengers.

Charlie elected to motor back to Cairns with Keith and Garry Wayne, the boat punching into the seas the whole way. They camped again on Night Island, and Charlie speared a six-pound painted cray for their supper, a skill he had learned from Kim. The next day they backtracked to Annie River for more fuel, but the wind and billows ate up the petrol, and they took refuge at Flinders Island, nowhere close to Cairns. Garry Wayne had developed nasty boils and burns on his legs from riding bareback in the heat and humidity. He used what little fuel was left in the engines to chase down a freighter crossing Bathurst Bay and begged a lift. When the captain declined to haul up the boat, Keith said he would stay aboard and hope for a tow. Charlie made sure the captain agreed to see that Garry Wayne got medical attention and then joined Keith for the wait. The freighter delivered Garry Wayne to Cairns the next morning, where a police launch picked him up and escorted him to hospital. As for Charlie and Keith, after a couple hungry days, they flagged down a sailboat with two men from New Guinea, who dragged them to Cairns. Another near disaster averted.

When he recuperated, Garry Wayne advised Charlie that the Pascoe River property was more than Charlie would be able to handle, even with his help. There were no roads into Cape York, and driving to the Pascoe, if it were even possible, would require weeks of supplies, good reliable vehicles, lots of guts and a great deal of luck. As far as he could see, it was a bad bet.

But the land was gorgeous. In spite of Garry Wayne's evaluation, Charlie waited to hear from his father. If the other Dean men were willing to give it a go, he'd make it happen somehow. In the end, though, the letter from Big Howard said he had no intention of investing in land on Cape York, and Charlie's younger brothers were not at all interested in Australia. Howard, always supportive, was willing to go in with him, again offering Charlie his entire chunk of inheritance, but Charlie sensed that Howard was just being a good brother. Besides, without the financial help of the other Deans, he'd still be short of the goal. Charlie had counted on that land as a sort of test for himself. He wanted to show that he was capable of setting up a venture bigger than Rosebud—even bigger than Bloomfield. Of course he was idealistic, but what great innovations had ever been made without idealism? His father was a realist, and Charlie heard Big Howard's voice echoing across the ocean—a theory isn't enough, you've got to articulate a plan. So what was the plan now? Maybe he should go back to New York and make peace with his father. On the other hand, he wasn't ready to give up the opportunities he had on this side of the Pacific. He was itching to make a move. The question was which direction now?

CHAPTER 20

Native Soil

Another year gone—so swift, so full.

—Gayle Hannah
from the Rosebud Farm journal

In March 1974, President Nixon declared, "I am not a crook." When he finally released the Watergate transcripts, the public was shocked at his use of foul language. "Expletive deleted" became a household expression. The tapes also incriminated him in the Watergate scandal. In July, the House Judiciary Committee adopted the first three Articles of Impeachment, charging Nixon with misuse of power and violation of his oath of office.

When impeachment became inevitable, Harry watched as Nixon gave a televised address to the nation announcing his resignation. On the morning of August 9, he delivered his farewell to the White House and then boarded a helicopter. An era of corruption, deception, and political dissent had come to a close.

Harry had rented a room from a family near Meadowbrook Orchards and had started working for his brother-in-law. The day began at 7:30 a.m., with a fifteen-minute coffee break and a half hour for lunch, and ended at 4:30

p.m., unless Harry was needed to drive jugs of cider into Boston to drop off at markets. He helped construct a building for the orchard store, he drove the flatbed truck through the trees collecting boxes of apples the Jamaican hired men had picked, and he chainsawed an acre for new planting. The hundred acres of Meadowbrook was all business, a far cry from Rosebud Farm, where the work was done at a leisurely pace and breaks were by free choice rather than by the clock. His brother-in-law's organization was competitive, and he was a demanding boss. Harry was learning from him about agriculture, carpentry and discipline.

One night a week, Harry played in a local men's hockey league. Other nights he strummed a guitar in his room, teaching himself songs or playing along with tapes. "May your hands always be busy,/ May your feet always be swift,/ May you have a strong foundation / When the winds of changes shift." Dylan's song reminded him of Kim, Rich and Charlie and his months on the farm. He hadn't heard from any of them in a while, and he missed the laughs and the companionship—he even missed the work. But there was plenty of work to be done on the apple orchard.

Occasionally he wandered over to the bunkhouse and relaxed with the Jamaicans. They always offered him a plate of rice and vegetables and a game or two of dominoes. On Friday, when the Jamaicans got paid, Harry drove them into town to shop for food and buy presents to send to their families, sharing in their good humor.

When Kim finally wrote, he said that Charlie had declined the Pascoe River property but had gone to Bloomfield, liked a piece of land for sale near Kim's Wyalla, and had given Broman a five-thousand-dollar deposit and a handshake agreement to buy the rest. But he had felt tentative about the arrangement. Before he made a full commitment, he was more than ever determined to take the Southeast Asia trip and go back to New York to see if he could change his brothers' minds about investing with him. Meanwhile, Charlie drove Kim to the Cairns airport in the farm truck to catch a flight back to Delaware. Hal Haskell's birthday was coming up in May, and Kim wanted to help him celebrate. When he shook Charlie's hand at the airport, Kim could not have known that it was the last time he would ever see his old school chum.

Charlie sojourned at Rosebud a while longer. Partially it was inertia that kept him there and partially it was Gayle. He could be himself with her. She knew how to dance his dance. She bore into him, opened him in a way that made him feel understood and safe. How strange it was to meet a woman on the other side of the world, one whose background was so different from his own. But even without the pricey education, she shared something with him, something ineffable yet undeniably pleasurable.

When Heather went into labor, Garry Wayne drove her to the hospital in Mareeba, where she gave birth to a daughter. The baby, named Rachel, changed the atmosphere at Rosebud. For Charlie, infant paraphernalia scattered about the Top House signaled that the time had come to leave. Finally he disengaged himself and took off for Darwin, planning eventually to catch a boat to Indonesia. Checking into a youth hostel, he thought he'd spend a little time in the city.

It is said that like minds attract, and when Charlie met Neil Sharman, he felt as if he had known the Australian for years. Neil worked for Northern Territory News in Darwin. His father, an executive in the newspaper industry in Sydney, had been influential in landing Neil the job.

Neil was two years younger than Charlie, and like Charlie he was an extrovert. Neil was also passionate about politics and world affairs. Energetic and athletic, he played soccer, cricket, rugby, water polo and basketball. He had a pied piper approach to life, and people were drawn to him because he played his own tune. One of the people he drew was Charlie Dean.

When Charlie suggested Neil travel to Southeast Asia with him, Neil immediately agreed. As a journalist, Neil must have known that the North Vietnamese troop numbers were believed to be at their highest levels ever. He must have heard that the South Vietnamese were girding themselves for a communist offensive. Already the communists had taken the Mekong Delta territory. Nevertheless, the day after Charlie enticed Neil into traveling with him, Neil walked into the newspaper office and resigned. He wrote to his friend Alex Klujin about the trip, inviting Alex and his wife to meet him in London in June. Neil would not make the rendezvous.

CHAPTER 21

Southeast Asia

Each of us has his own compass that tells us when we are off or on course.

—from the Rosebud Farm journal

n May, a freighter departed from Darwin. Charlie and Neil were aboard, sleeping on deck, using their packs as pillows. They docked in Timor, where rugged mountains rose along an aqua coast and fishermen cast nets into the sea. In the countryside, women walked from villages with jugs of water or bundled husks of corn balanced atop their heads. Farmers worked water buffaloes in rice paddies, prodding them gently with long sticks. The children were beautiful. Dark-skinned, their wide mouths smiling with white teeth, they looked a mix of Asian and Portuguese, whose seventeenth century missions stood as monuments to colonialism.

Charlie and Neil were eager for travel and did not hang around Timor long. They hopped boats to Jawa and Jacarta and moved on into Sumatra, traveling overland by crowded bus, hitchhiking when they could and walking much of the way. The people of Indonesia were friendly, offering the strangers fruit or bowls of rice. The language was not difficult to learn and with a combination of English, a few

Indonesian words, and hand signals, they were able to find their way around.

But the rest of Southeast Asia awaited. Even though they were making their own timetable, Charlie felt the pinch of time. The year he'd spent at Rosebud Farm had gone by in a blink, and the next six months no doubt would fly by. Yet already he missed the farm. On the other hand, there would be much to tell his friends when he saw them again. He owed it to Neil to make sure they had experiences they would never forget.

On the first of June, they caught a boat to Malaysia, stopping briefly in Singapore, a big, dirty city, before making their way to Kuala Lumpur by train, bus, and thumbing rides.

Charlie was as indifferent to Kuala Lumpur as its concrete seemed toward him. He had grown up in a big city, but in the last year he'd changed, and he wanted nothing to do with urban hustle. He urged Neil on to Thailand.

Along the way they stopped at markets, and Charlie bought candlefruit nuts for Rich. For Heather he purchased two small wood carvings to honor her becoming a mother—a fertility pig and a female figure holding an urn between her legs. For Gayle, he dickered over a Buddha head. When they reached Bangkok, Charlie sent the gifts along with letters, promising Gayle he would see her again at Rosebud.

In Bangkok rooms and food were cheap. The people were hospitable and spoke enough English to make their stay comfortable. The young men decided to make the city their base from which they would make trips to Cambodia and Laos, returning to Bangkok to plan the rest of their route. Charlie was eager to see the Buddhist temples, and Neil wanted to absorb the culture. They were both glad to get away from their routines and optimistic about what lay ahead of them.

Thailand's rains were still a month away and when Charlie and Neil trekked north, they found the landscape scruffy and dry. It was the burning season, when fields were cleared of debris from the harvest, and the land lay under a perpetual gray haze. They found their way to San Chai, several hours' walk from the nearest road and one of the oldest villages in Thailand. Bamboo huts littered dusty hilltops and Akha tribespeople, bronze men with ponytails or shaven heads, chopped at fields of bamboo. Beautiful women wrapped in black-beaded and embroidered cloth were adorned with heavy silver necklaces and bracelets.

None of the Akha villagers knew even a little English, and a native escorted Charlie and Neil to the chief, who spoke a bit of broken English. The chief was about Charlie's age and invited the newcomers to dine in his hut with a few other citizens from the village. They folded their legs on the dirt floor around a cooking fire. In a corner a man sat cross-legged, one hand on a rifle across his knees. He kept his eyes on the strangers but said nothing. Charlie didn't like guns. He would not make any moves that would give the man in the corner a reason to raise his rifle.

The men scooped rice from a pot, pressed it into little balls and tossed the rice pellets into their mouths, and Charlie and Neil imitated the process, smiling and gesturing thanks. At one point a scrawny chicken scurried across the floor. One man grabbed it and twisted its head, plucked its feathers and set it to roast over the fire intact—comb, feet and all. When he deemed it done, he heaved a cleaver into the bird, splintering bones over the ground, and then tossed the pieces into the pot to enhance the meal.

As darkness fell, the other guests departed, leaving Neil and Charlie with the chief and a man who looked to be in his forties. The man lit a candle and an opium lamp and then took to a straw mat next to the chief. The ancestors of

the older man, the chief said, had fled from the armies of
Kublai Khan. With his high cheekbones, his gleaming black
eyes and shining shock of black hair, he might in another
time have been a Mongol warrior.

With clean, easy motions, the man twirled a clump
of opium on a needle over the low flame, occasionally com-
pressing it gently between thumb and forefinger. When he
had a mass the size and consistency of a rabbit pellet, he
pressed the stuff into the small bowl of the chief's pipe.
The chief tilted the bowl over the flame, drawing hard and
evenly. The opium sputtered and bubbled like melting molasses,
and clouds of sweet, pungent smoke rose up slowly to the
thatch of the roof.

Several times on previous evenings Charlie had
passed up opportunities to smoke opium, but now he was
lured by the flickering lamplight of the bamboo hut and the
dark Akha men who had spent nights observing this ritual
for the last thousand years.

He drew on the pipe and liked the saccharine taste.
He accepted another invitation to puff from the pipe, and
then another. Lying on a mat, he sank into a warm glow and
fell asleep.

The following evening the ceremony was repeated,
but on the third night, Charlie excused himself. He was feeling weak from the sweltering heat, a single meal a day, and
the effects of the drug. Neil seemed glad to retreat, too.
Besides, Cambodia awaited them.

For the last year, the Khmer Rouge army had attacked supply
boats coming along the Mekong River from South Vietnam
into Cambodia's capital. When their attempts were foiled,
first by the rainy season and then by counterattacks, the
Khmer Rouge altered their tactics. Instead of concentrating
on breaking the lines of communication into Phnom Penh,

they terrorized the city and its inhabitants with artillery fire and 107mm rockets. It appeared for a while that these attacks against civilians would succeed. But once again the Cambodian government withstood the barrage and the capital held, albeit with a delicate grip. When the dry season came to a close in June, the Khmer Rouge maintained a tight stranglehold on Phnom Penh, but without a victory.

Charlie was wary about entering Phnom Penh in late July, but he had heard the city was now quiet and, besides, he had committed himself to seeing the wreckage. It was one thing to talk about war; it was another to stand at its center and feel the hostility. To Charlie, it was obvious that the U.S. was still involved in the conflict, if not with soldiers, then by supplying weapons and ammunition, half of which were sold to the Khmer Rouge. Charlie had read that the 1973 Paris Agreement included a ban on infiltration of arms or personnel to reinforce North Vietnamese troops in the South, as well as a ban on the use of Laotian or Cambodian territory for that purpose, but the U.S. was allowed to continue to supply arms to the army of the Republic of Vietnam. It looked like the Paris Agreement was no more than a piece of paper.

The streets of Phnom Penh resembled a war-torn migrant camp. The Cambodians were friendly, but when Charlie attempted to ask a few if they knew what the civil war was about, they had no idea. Neither did the Laotian refugees, even though they were the war's victims. At night Charlie and Neil tried to sleep through the booming of artillery fired across the Mekong. Had everyone in the U.S. forgotten about the war—or were they too caught up in the Watergate hearings to care? Did Americans know that their own government was encouraging the fighting by supplying both sides with weapons? The situation was not only ridiculous, but it smelled to Charlie of genocide.

Charlie wrote to Garry Wayne, encouraging him to come to Cambodia and make use of his building skills to help the people get their country back together. Cambodia could use Garry Wayne's native intelligence and courage. All Charlie himself had were his verbal abilities, which did him little good with the language barrier. Garry Wayne might make a difference, even in a small way. Garry Wayne wrote back, but Charlie never received his letters.

When Neil and Charlie returned to Bangkok, Charlie admitted that the road was beginning to wear on him. He had thought he might be able to lend a hand to the people of war-torn areas, but he hadn't expected to be overwhelmed by their desperate circumstances and the crushing futility they felt. What little encouragement he and Neil brought them was swallowed up by the threat of another surge of violence. It was time to think about themselves.

In a letter to Harry, Charlie said that he would be leaving Bangkok the next day for Laos and would most likely be gone a month. Then he and Neil would stop back in Bangkok before heading on to Nepal. "But if it gets cold before I finally leave Bangkok, I may zip back to my chooks," he wrote. He was still thinking about Rosebud, still tempted to come back to the farm. Again he said he "proba-bly/maybe" would be in the States by Christmas and would get in touch. He ended the letter with, "Take care and stay warm in your heart. With love, Charlie."

The subtext of "if" and "may" and "probably" indicated that Charlie was having reservations about this journey. Something was telling him he was on the wrong path. Just before he left Bangkok, he penned an enigmatic, troubling letter to Kim. True to form, Charlie's syntax was eloquent and animated, but Kim puzzled over the contents. It was as if Charlie were trying to sort out some conflict among his intellect, his intuition, and his heart. The letter read:

> *There once was a young man with two perfectly good heads. He was sort of proud—after all, two heads are better than one—and he was sort of bummed out because he had the hardest time making decisions. He had a successful youth and did many things that most people with just one head only dream of. He went on a trip, and one head sort of lost interest, and the other head, previously described as uninspired, or at least under-developed, started to bloom. And it told the heart (there was only one) to feel its best ever because here were friends and love that the other head had never imagined. But just as the two heads reached equilibrium, the education ended. The examination had begun and continues to this day. The young man continues to roam and, as in all good examinations, he is learning while he is being tested. And both heads are doing marvelously well. Too well, in fact. Decisions don't come easily except a decision by the heart not to choose. For the heart loves both heads equally and has been touched in return by both. There is a happy ending, but it is not written. For the heart is comforted by the words of a brother, "It will happen, that's cool, just let it happen." And so it will, my brothers, because above all, peace and love and wisdom and harmony will be served.*
>
> *Love to you all, Charlie.*

Charlie felt he was being tested by the pilgrimage, and his answer to the test was not to make a decision but to "just let it happen." In spite of his self-examination, Charlie still believed things would turn out well for him. But he seemed to be trying too hard to convince himself. Nothing he had seen so far indicated a happy ending for anyone.

A first postscript to the letter indicated that he and Neil would be in Bangkok until August 22, and thereafter Charlie could be reached in care of American Peace Corps in Kamaldi, Nepal. A second postscript wished a happy birthday to the Leos at Rosebud, and a third gave the warning, "Watch out for those babies."

Both Harry and Kim understood that Charlie was pigheaded and that he would follow through with the trip because he was involved in it now. Using his wit and his eloquence, he had always been able to handle any situation. There was no reason to worry.

Once known as Lan Xang, land of the million elephants, Laos was under the control of various warlords until the 1820s, when it was overtaken by Siam, now Thailand. Shortly afterward, France acquired all land east of the Mekong River, including Laos, and united the local provinces under one principality. French civil servants built grand estates in Luang Prabang and Vientiane, which still stand as monuments to colonial history, but not much else besides thick coffee and remnants of French phrases remain of France's influence.

During World War II, the Japanese invaded Indochina and in 1945 the French again liberated the region. Shortly thereafter, the Pathet Lao formed, using weapons supplied by the Soviets. In 1961, the United States threatened military intervention to halt the spread of communism and the following year launched an unpublicized war against the Pathet Lao, who allied themselves with North Vietnam communists. That war would last until just months before Charlie and Neil entered Laos. Although Charlie had an inkling about the American political and economic scene, there was not much news about U.S. activities in Southeast Asia. If he and Neil knew of the recent unrest, they chose to ignore it and walk straight into the turmoil.

On the pavement of the ancient royal capital Luang Prabang, Buddhist monks knelt in their orange robes as they had done for centuries to receive offerings of food from the townspeople. Luang Prabang, reputed to be the most beautiful city in Southeast Asia, was named for the gold image of Buddha, the Prabang. The seat of Lao culture, the city was decorated with exquisitely carved Buddhist temples and breathtaking natural beauty.

Situated at the junction of the Nom Khan and Mekong rivers, Luang Prabang moved at a slow, sleepy pace, even with a population of two hundred thousand people. Surrounded by the peaceful spirit of the Buddhists, Charlie felt drawn to the city. Except for the China-capped soldiers with machine guns under arms or slung on their backs, he might have been enticed to stay. But in the eyes of the soldiers, he could see there was something fomenting.

Nevertheless, he and Neil idled their time. They treated themselves to dinner at a restaurant, ordering chateaubriand, beans, carrots, and French bread, accompanied by beer, wine and coffee. After dozens of plates of fried rice and bowls of noodle soup, the taste of good steak brought them nearly to tears of pleasure. The bill amounted to $1.75 each, after which Neil lit a cigarette, sat back in his chair, and smiled at their good fortune. Other nights they alternated beef Bourguignon with delicious venison. Mekong whisky was thirty cents a pint, and a pack of cigarettes made from American tobacco cost a dime. Sixteen fat, ready-rolled reefers could be had for seven cents.

For a week they indulged themselves and then headed down to Vientiane, where the crushing heat drove them into an American library to read old issues of *Sports Illustrated*. They checked into a hotel, a creaky old wooden relic from French colonial days that took up a half a city block and boasted long concrete verandahs with large shuttered windows.

Most days they arose at nine in the morning, took a shower under a pathetic drizzle that faintly resembled plumbing, and wandered down to a café for croissants and coffee. From noon until after five they sipped Mekong whiskey or forty-cent Heinekens, when finally it was cool enough to walk around back streets lined with old villas and fan palms or down to the end of the Avenue Lan Xang to Monument-aux-Morts, a garish mockery of L'Arc de Triomphe. Because it was built with cement donated by the U.S. government to expand the airstrip at Wattay Airport, the monument was known as "the vertical runway."

At the marketplace, Meo tribespeople sold their hand woven material, Indians offered bolts of voile and silk, Vietnamese displayed black silk and Chinaware, and Laotian merchants loitered over silver and gold brocade items. All the vendors chatted and gossiped with none of the hustling or hawking of wares common in the rest of Asia.

Across from the market stood the compound of the Pathet Lao, well barricaded and guarded. The Pathet Lao troops, identified by their Chinese caps and baggy trousers, browsed through the market or along the streets, some wearing the green arm bands of the Coalition Army. Except for the ever-present machine guns, they seemed little threat to the marketplace.

It is said that Laos is not a place but a state of mind. In spite of the presence of the soldiers, Charlie fell into what the French refer to as "*malaise Laotian*," a lethargy that robs one of ambition to do more than linger in cafes all day. This state of torpor produces a sort of forgetfulness where conflict or peril seems a vague afterthought. But the seduction of this malaise makes a man vulnerable. He relaxes his guard and reverts to old, comfortable habits. For Charlie, those habits included speaking his mind and enjoying a good argument, and he engaged Neil in impassioned conversations. But on the street he held his tongue. Even Charlie sensed that one did not argue with the Pathet Lao.

Days of inactivity brought on the rumblings of restlessness, and finally they made a decision to move on toward Thakhek. But how to get there? The roads were abominable. After debate, they decided that the most efficient and logical mode of transportation was a ferry boat down the Mekong.

CHAPTER 22

Pathet Lao

The Sanctum Sanctorum is the chamber of your own heart.

—from Harry's journal

As the ferry boat engine started, Charlie watched the boat leave the shore. A guard yanked his hands behind him, tied his wrists with rope, and looped the rope around his neck. Charlie had to keep his elbows bent to relieve the pressure on his throat. He had no idea what had happened to his backpack. He no longer cared about his camera. Somewhere along his travels he was told that Asians believe a picture taken with a camera deprives them of something precious and personal that cannot be recovered. Charlie had scoffed, refusing to believe such nonsense. He wished now that he had taken the admonition more seriously.

Neil was somewhere behind him. When Charlie called out to him, a guard struck his back with the butt of a gun and pushed him along a narrow path through the jungle. Charlie stumbled forward, the rope nearly choking him. He struggled to free himself from the chafing at his neck. Rifle fire exploded over his head and he ducked. His ears ringing, he realized how easily a bullet could go into his back.

A month earlier, while they traveled through South-east Asia, Charlie and Neil had learned that President Nixon had resigned from office. But now, as they were driven through a rainforest at gunpoint, they had no way of knowing that President Gerald Ford had pardoned Nixon for all criminal acts perpetrated while he was in office and that Ford had pledged to continue with Nixon's foreign policy, a policy that now personally affected them. Charlie had led opposition to the war in Southeast Asia not only because he disagreed with the aggression on principle but also to speak for the poor bastards on the front lines who took lead, lost limbs, and gave up their lives for Nixon's war. Now he felt a strange thrill in knowing this was what it must feel like to face the enemy. When he returned to the States, he'd have a better idea of what was at stake. When he got involved in political action again, it would mean even more.

They walked for an hour. Two hours. Three. Charlie grew tired, and when he slowed down to rest, a soldier thumped him in the back with the rifle.

The jungle was hot, and he was thirsty. "*Koi yak deum nam,*" he thought were the words. He was given no water.

The heat was nearly unbearable, and leeches that hung in wait from lower leaves along the trail attached themselves to his legs.

When they passed through a village, it appeared deserted. The residents perhaps had retreated to their houses, small huts on stilts. Charlie had heard that villagers could be arrested for helping prisoners.

When night fell, the procession stopped. Charlie fell to the ground in exhaustion. One of the guards started a fire, and he was able to see Neil, whose hands also were tied. Neil looked brave, and Charlie assumed that soon they would arrive at a military headquarters where they would be questioned. When the leaders discovered the mistake, that Neil and Charlie were no threat, surely they would be released. That was the logical process. It couldn't be long before they reached someone in authority. Certainly they would be reasonable people.

The guards set rice to boil in a pot over the fire. One of them untied Charlie's hands, and he rubbed his sore shoulders and picked the leeches from his legs. He was given a small bowl of rice and a drink of water. Although he was tempted to refuse the food, he saw that Neil was eating and realized he may need his strength. While he scooped rice with his fingers, a guard kept a rifle leveled at his head. Charlie appraised his captors, five men who looked to range in age from thirteen to twenty, younger even than Neil and years younger than Charlie. The absurdity of the situation almost made him laugh.

But there was no laughing when guards drove stakes into the ground and tied them hand and foot for the night. As the fire died down, the insects grew murderous and without a free hand to swat them, the young men were tortured by bites and stings. When a guard lit an opium pipe, the smoke offered some relief from the attacks. Finally the Laotians slept, and Charlie and Neil assessed their situation in whispers. Charlie tried to apologize for not giving up the camera, but Neil said the Pathet Lao would have found another excuse to take them into custody. They agreed that they were most likely to be used as a commodity, a trade for something. When the trade was complete, they would be let go. They encouraged each other, both of them trying to keep positive. They will be freed tomorrow, they told each other—they had no doubt.

Morning dawned with a steamy heat. The two men were wrenched to their feet and ropes again were tied around their hands and necks. Without breakfast, the march began again. Even if Charlie could have gotten free, he wouldn't have known which way to go. It seemed as if they had been moving in a large circle, perhaps to confuse him. If there were landmarks, he had not seen them.

He tried to reason with a guard, using the sense of entitlement he had grown to abhor. "*Koi ma chak Amaeleeka.*" I am from America, he said, as if this announcement would impress the boy. He knew that the Pathet Lao considered themselves at war with the U.S. and with all Americans, but Charlie felt responsible for getting Neil into this situation and he'd try anything to get them out of it. The soldier answered quickly in angry Lao words and thrust Charlie forward.

After another day of marching, they came to a cave. It appeared that families had been living here, maybe to avoid the barrage of bombs. Charlie had seen caves on mountainsides, no doubt all occupied by soldiers or civilians. Some caves had been bombed and the openings filled with rubble. American bombs. He wondered if people had been trapped inside.

They were allowed to rest and a guard gave them water. Charlie had gotten used to having a rifle barrel aimed constantly at his chest or head, but he was incensed. He could see no reason for this injustice. Nothing in his pack suggested he was working for the U.S. government— nothing suggested he was a soldier or a spy. This detour was not on the schedule. People would be waiting to hear from them. Certainly someone would come to free them.

As they hiked farther into the jungle, Charlie felt the situation growing more grave. He had no idea how grave until they arrived at a camp surrounded by a high fence of bamboo stalks, the tops sharpened to points. Two primitive bamboo huts with thatched roofs made up the camp. The best Charlie could figure, they were somewhere between Pak Sane and Thakhek. Guards shoved them through a doorway into one of the huts and pushed them to the dirt floor. Their feet were locked into wooden blocks, their wrists untied and fasted into handcuffs.

Charlie was surprised to find other prisoners in the hut—an American, a Chinese, a Thai. They spoke English, which brought Charlie great relief. When he learned that the men had been held in the camp for two years, some even longer, he refused at first to believe them. More prisoners occupied the other hut, held hostage for just as long—all MIAs. He felt as if he were in a dream and would awaken in his bunk at Rosebud Farm any minute. He would go to breakfast at the Top House and banter with the other farmers about weeds and seedlings. But the stench in the hut was too real—acrid body odor, urine and shit. It was the smell of dread and despair. The ratted hair and full beards of the men and the effects of hunger and illness on their faces and bodies convinced Charlie that they spoke the truth. Suddenly he felt a mortal fear.

At first the other hostages were suspicious, even jealous of the newcomers, who were healthy, and, until recently, well fed. The men suffered from malnutrition, and some had malaria and intestinal parasites. It took days for Charlie and Neil to be accepted into their odd fraternity. The prisoners pumped them for news of the outside, for any indication that freedom might be near. Charlie consoled and reassured, although his assurance was not based on any knowledge.

The prisoners whispered among themselves so as not to draw the attention of the guards. The other men said that if they caused trouble, they had no doubt they would be eliminated. Other prisoners had disappeared with guards into the jungle and had not returned.

It didn't take long for Charlie to learn the daily routine. He was let out of the blocks to use the latrine and to eat. On good days he was given all the rice he could eat, sometimes flavored with fish. When supplies ran low, he was restricted to a single meal of rice a day. Every minute out of the stocks, a gun was aimed at him. He tried to make eye contact with one of the younger guards, thinking that he could forge a connection of mutual humanity. But the guard refused to look into Charlie's eyes. It occurred to Charlie that the guard, too, was being watched.

Some of the prisoners were allowed to tend a small garden of tapioca and mustard greens, and Charlie helped with the gardening, always under the eye of a rifle barrel. In those brief moments, he thought of Rosebud, where the farmers were tending fields of soybeans and planning a market trip to Cairns. He felt close to Kim and Rich when he was in the garden, and he wondered if they thought of him.

In the hut, Charlie tried to build bonds with the other men. They spoke about their favorite meals, of girl-friends and sports events. They imagined cold glasses of beer. They talked of home. Sometimes they cried. At other times they prayed. At Rosebud Charlie had simplified his life to basic needs, a lifestyle far removed from his closet of preppy clothes and shelves of books in East Hampton. But now the catalogue was reduced to a bowl, one pair of tattered pants and a pair of shoes left outside the hut. The fine china of his Manhattan upbringing, the silver teapots of St. George's—did they still exist, or had he imagined them?

Nights were dark and filled with noises of insects and frogs. Ironically, mornings sometimes broke as lovely as dawns on Long Island. How odd to think of that life now, where men rose from sleep with bright hope for the day. Charlie thought about what brought him to this place. Was it his reckless vitality? His stubbornness? His naïve trust in decency? And should he resent his education or his hours on the country club tennis court or the money his father had bequeathed him, which was of no value to him now?

He envisioned his mother sitting at home, waiting to hear from him. She seemed so close, and the image of her comforted him even in so desolate a place. He would have given anything for a chance to sit at the table and argue with his father again. His father's anger, which Charlie so easily roused and which he undoubtedly deserved, seemed foolish to him now. He longed to listen to music. To dance and laugh. To hold a woman and smell the perfume of her hair mixed with compost, earth, bread and tropical flowers. He wanted to feel the dizzy complacency that he thought back then would never end. In order to keep himself steady, he had to live each moment without remembering, without expecting, without hoping. To look back was to be plunged into desperation—a hazard he couldn't afford.

As weeks wore on, Charlie measured the passing of hours by the movement of shadows across the ground. On rainy days, time stood still. Only the smells and sounds changed. There was a tentative hopefulness in the morning call of a bird or the croak of a frog, a scentless stillness at noon in anticipation of a bowl of rice, a few grains of which were cause for celebration. At night a party of bugs, reptiles and amphibians gathered, their noises rising and falling almost like breath. It was their silence that was most disturbing, a hyphen of waiting for some coming of bad news.

Every day the prisoners weighed their chances of breaking free, all possibilities unquestionably slim. The fellow hostages were military men, trained to deal with the prospect of capture. A Code of Conduct devised by the Defense Department had set standards for GIs that included resisting by all means available and making every effort to escape and to help other prisoners escape. Charlie accepted that if these men in the past two years had not been able to fight their way to freedom, freedom did not exist. Besides, the thick jungle, mountains with razor sharp rocks, insects, snakes, leeches and hungry predators offered no more promise than the guards' guns.

Neither Charlie nor Neil had the training—physical or psychological—to help them deal with the conditions they faced. Much of the time, Charlie experienced boredom. In his worst moments, he tried to lift himself by recalling obstacles he had overcome, like the trip over the Sierra Nevadas in Omnibus when he nearly gave up and Howard made him keep going. He thought of his brothers, and these thoughts gave him strength. No matter what happened, Charlie vowed to hold onto his spiritual faith and the desire to find some purpose for himself in the world. These two qualities, both of which he embraced with all his heart, sustained him.

In the months that passed, Charlie's and Neil's parents contacted both the United States and Australian governments to report their disappearance. Both governments filed objections to the detentions, insisting that the young men were merely tourists. Both embassies tried to secure their release, but the Pathet Lao authorities denied knowledge either of their capture or of their whereabouts. But neither Charlie nor Neil had any way to know of the efforts to emancipate them. What they did learn was that the Pathet Lao were unpredictable and that there was no way for them to be sure about what was planned for them.

The prisoners talked of the Geneva Conventions, of the international rule that sick prisoners must be released and that they must be protected from abuse. They spoke of the possibility of being handed over to North Vietnam. Maybe they would be assigned to the Hanoi Hilton, a propaganda showplace. At least there they would be allowed to shave twice a week and wash their clothing. They would be fed vegetables, bread and enough rice to keep them from starving. If they were to remain in prison, Hanoi would be a better choice than this rainforest.

By Charlie's best estimates, it was mid December when he and Neil were taken from their hut and marched again through the dense forest. He dared to hope this meant they were about to be released, but when he heard something about Vietnam, he suspected that his captors had decided to give them over to the Viet Cong.

Eventually they were led to a rutted road, no more than two parallel paths through woods. By the sun, they had been traveling north. If they continued in this direction, they would enter North Vietnam within a couple of days. It was good to be out of the forest at least, even though bomb craters along the trail showed evidence that the path was used as a supply route. Charlie wondered if this was the Ho Chi Minh trail and if the craters were made by some of the two million tons of bombs dropped from American planes in the last decade, more explosives than fell on Germany and all of occupied Europe during World War II. And yet the road had remained open.

Some soldiers came toward them, waving and speaking rapidly. They shook their heads and brandished their weapons. Up ahead was a small shack, no bigger than a closet, and the soldiers motioned toward it. In the months that the young Pathet Lao guard had held his rifle at Charlie's heart, never had he learned as much as the man's name. Now the guard looked Charlie in the eye for the first time, and Charlie knew what lay ahead.

He wondered what it was these men understood about Neil Sharman and Charlie Dean that they could pass such judgment on them. And who would find them? They carried no card, no way to identify themselves, no way to prove that they had ever existed.

As guards pressed them into the shed, Charlie felt old, as if in twenty-four years he had lived a long life. By some measure he had lived long and well—better than most of the people in the world. But none of what he had been given mattered now. In a few days it would be Christmas, and he thought how his family would celebrate without him again this year. But he couldn't worry about that. All that mattered was this moment, this quiet darkness with Neil beside him. He put an arm around his friend.

Charlie heard the rifle fire before he felt the bullets slam into his chest. He hoped that in the fog of morning he would see a star.

CHAPTER 23

The true goal of life is to return to the source from which we have come.

—from Harry's journal

Harry spent the winter crating apples at Meadowbrook Orchards. He received a letter from Kim, who was worried that he hadn't gotten a letter from Charlie in months and asked if Harry had had any word from him. Maybe Charlie had arrived in the States without coming back to Australia. Harry had heard nothing, but he had a bad feeling. It wasn't like Charlie to disappear. Charlie's greatest loyalty was to his friends. He'd have communicated if he were able to. Kim was afraid that he'd gotten into some trouble, maybe gotten tied up with the wrong people. Harry wrote back that surely Charlie knew how to take care of himself, although he couldn't convince himself of the truth of that statement. Charlie may have been slow to make a decision, but once he made it he drove ahead full steam. Harry hoped Charlie hadn't headed in the wrong direction.

The apples were blooming with spring blossoms when Dave came to the cider house and told Harry that his mother was on the phone to speak to him. She knew better than to call during work hours; Dave liked him to be on task when he was paying an hourly wage. But Dave said it was important. Lea and Phil Reynolds knew the Deans from St. George's, where Phil and Big Howard were both on the board of trustees. Lea said she had just gotten off the phone with Charlie's mother, Andree. Charlie had been killed in Laos. She didn't have many details, something about Charlie being held prisoner and futile attempts to get him released. Then the execution. She knew Harry would want to know.

Harry told Dave he couldn't work that afternoon. He didn't want to be alone, but the Jamaicans had gone home and weren't due back until mid-summer to get ready for the harvest. He thought about going to Wenham to be with his family, but that didn't seem right. More than anything he wanted to be at Rosebud, sitting with his buddies at the Top House, consoling each other and trying to figure out what had gone so very wrong.

He went back to his room and thought about Howard, imagining how he must be feeling, how he'd feel himself if he'd lost one of his own brothers. He thought about Charlie asking him to go with him to Southeast Asia and how he'd declined. Things might have been different if he'd gone. But he couldn't blame himself. Charlie had wanted to strike out on his own, and he had done that. Whatever happened to him, he must have known that he had to take responsibility for his actions and what the consequences of those actions might be.

Harry put on some music. Then he wept. When he was empty, he thought about the dream of owning land that he and Charlie had shared. Now more than ever he would work toward that dream. Kim and Rich had sown the seeds, but Charlie's passion had fueled it. And when he got it—the piece of acreage, the house he would build himself, the family he would raise on that property—when the dream became reality, Harry would think of Charlie as he sat on the porch with a cigar looking out at what he had done. And he would raise a glass to his Rosebud brother.

Hal Haskell also knew the Deans through St. George's. When Hal heard that Charlie had been captured, he had used his influences to try to get him released, without success.

Gayle responded to the news of Charlie's capture by writing in the Rosebud journal:

Where are you, laughing one?
Sitting in the mud, in pain?
Oh, my mind has eyes
but they cannot break the dark....
Honey mouth, sly-dog eyes
white, white teeth,
Oh, Charlie, I've shared dreams with you.
What hurts, really hurts
is that I cannot share this nightmare, too.
Oh, power of love,
speed of brotherhood,
send me to you
and you back home to us.

But Charlie was not to come back. The final news came to Australia in a letter from Kim's father. Kim was spun into a confusion he was at a loss to sort out. He turned to the Rosebud journal and tried to press some reason from his pen.

The daring walker of the tightrope
knows his thin line chances.
The diver of the deep blue
is aware of Mother Nature's random choices.
The cliff climber or the snow skier,
they too are aware of the thin line they travel.

But what of innocence? What of brotherhood?
Did Charlie walk the chalk?
Did he balance over the net knowingly?
Is his fate born from innocence or ignorance?
Is innocence a crime?

This was a man of innocence, not a man of war.

Kim had known Charlie since they were fourteen years old. He always believed that Charlie would run for public office, and he was convinced that Charlie would have won election and that he would have been an honest and dedicated leader. Should he hold America and the hostilities in Southeast Asia responsible for Charlie's death? Or was it Charlie's own naiveté in thinking himself invulnerable? But finding fault was not going to bring him back. Surely in those last months, Charlie, with his spiritual strength, was an inspiration for his fellow prisoners. In that case, he had finally found a way to do some real good.

Kim read again Charlie's letter about having two heads. He knew there are two kinds of intelligence. Once is acquired from books and collected information. With such knowledge one rises in the world and is ranked behind or ahead of others. The other kind of intelligence is inborn and overflows into every action. This intelligence is pure and fluid; it surges from the heart as well as the head. Charlie was rich with this second kind of knowing. He might have ignored the dangers around him, but in his heart he knew exactly what he was doing. His only desire had been to make a difference in the world. Surely Charlie had made a difference at Rosebud.

Kim knew that Charlie had been deeply devout. At St. George's School he had volunteered for the Acolytes Guild not out of a sense of duty or affinity for ceremony but because he felt it an honor to assist the chaplains at the daily services. His faith had no haughtiness about it, and Kim had no doubt that his faith sustained him in his final weeks. At Rosebud, Charlie had talked about the Buddhists he'd met in Japan and how Buddhists believe they choose the time and place of their own deaths. Perhaps, Kim thought, Charlie had chosen his.

AFTERWORD

When Harry and I visited Rosebud Farm in July 2004, Rich had transformed the bunkhouse into comfortable living quarters with a modern kitchen. Although the bathroom was still an outhouse, it had running water and a flush toilet. We asked to see the Top House, and Rich led us up the hill through jagged blades of Guinea grass six feet tall riddled with paralytic ticks. The Guinea grass seeds had blown onto the property from a neighbor's land and had taken over the field Kim used to keep neatly mowed in front of the Top House. Once we reached the house, we worked our way delicately over rotting porch floorboards to the interior. Inside, the floor was peppered with mouse droppings. The piano was gone, the kitchen stripped of supplies. On one counter sat two quart jars of pickled tomatoes Anni had canned when she came with Kim to Rosebud. The jars were dated 1975. A listing bookshelf held a few moldy books—*Cosmic Consciousness, Stranger in a Strange Land*, a handbook of first aid, *Reader's Digest* condensed classics of *The Three Musketeers, Moby Dick* and *Hard Times*. A tall window still bore a painted landscape, and red and blue light filtered through, dancing on the dusty floor. It was obvious that nothing now lived at the Top House but mice, most likely pythons who fed on them, and definitely ghosts.

At the close of 1973, when the Vietnam War officially ended, nearly sixty thousand Americans, 1.2 million North Vietnamese and Viet Cong, and two million civilians had died. To date, two thousand Americans are listed as missing from the Vietnam War. Using information gathered from informants, mostly Lao, the U.S. government has spent thirty years piecing together likely sites where Americans are buried or where planes or helicopters carrying Americans may have crashed. The task has been complicated because much of the U.S. war effort in Laos, aimed primarily at cutting off communist Vietnamese supply lines that ran through the country, was covert.

Since the Vietnam War ended, investigators have recovered and identified seven hundred sets of remains. Hundreds of others have been recovered but have yet to be identified. Among those identified are Neil Sharman and Charles Maitland Dean.

Today Harry Reynolds lives on his land in Vermont near his friend Sam Burr. Kim Haskell and his partner Anni tend their fruit trees at Wyalla in Bloomfield. Kim has a new steel-hulled boat named Big Mama and charters tours along the Great Barrier Reef. Jeb Buck and Gayle Hannah live in Kuranda. Heather Smart and her daughter Rachel are in Cairns, and Garry Wayne lives in Herberton, Queensland. Rich Trapnell operates Rosebud Farm, an organic tree nursery in Kuranda.

Charlie Dean now rests in peace in Sag Harbor on the land his great-great grandfather claimed. But I believe a part of him still lingers under a midnight moon in Far North Queensland.

ACKNOWLEDGMENTS

I have many people to thank for help in writing this book. Memories spanning over thirty years fade, and had it not been for Harry's assiduous journaling, letter writing and picture taking, there would be no detail. Thanks to his mother, Lea Parson, for saving every letter he wrote from Australia. Loving gratitude to Kim Haskell for his animated stories, for connecting me with people involved with Rosebud Farm and for putting up Harry and me at Wyalla in Bloomfield. Thanks to Rich Trapnell for his eloquent emails and for a room (and outdoor shower) at Rosebud Farm. Gayle Hannah and Heather Smart supplied domestic color to the Rosebud scene, and Garry Wayne Thompson eloquently described the trip to the Pascoe River. Much gratitude goes to Joe Crarey, who went to Laos after Charlie disappeared and allowed me to use one of his letters to make projections about Charlie's experiences there. Web Golinkin and Sam Burr added memories about Harvard days. Gerry Cohen, Peter Caron and John Caron were helpful in opening doors to Charlie's years at UNC Chapel Hill, and the Carrboro anecdotes of Karen Ellis Gray and Don Wright found their way into the book. Thanks also to Debbie Dunn Murray for her memories of the tragic drowning of Dennis at Devil's Pool and to Tom Blagden for his recollections of Houghton Island. Hal Haskell was good enough to clarify his role in politics during that time. Special thanks to Alex Klujin for sending me his eulogy for Neil Sharman's memorial service.

Mountains of gratitude to my writing group—Margie Bekoff, Paul Forlenza, Ann Kensek, Christine Moriarty, Harriet Szanto and Cheryl Conner—for critique of drafts.

The help of my Spalding University colleagues, Luke Wallin, for his careful reading, Roy Hoffman, for early guidance, and Bob Finch, for advice about structure, was invaluable. Dana Barile's pictures of Laos and Vietnam gave me insight into the scenes in Southeast Asia. The Steerforth Press (2003) biography, *Howard Dean: A Citizen's Guide to the Man Who Would Be President*, offered a wealth of information about the lives of the Dean brothers. I am deeply indebted to Dieter Dengler's memoir, *Escape from Laos* (Presidio Press 1979). Hundreds of internet sources have been useful in researching this book.

Eternally grateful thanks go to Howard, Jim and Bill Dean for their help and encouragement for this project.

This book is dedicated to Kim, Rich, Harry, and especially to Charlie.